Michel

STUDIES IN CANADIAN LITERATURE

Michel Tremblay

Renate Usmiani

Douglas & McIntyre
VANCOUVER

This book has been published with the help of a grant from the Canadian
Federation for the Humanities, using funds provided by the Social
Sciences and Humanities Research Council of Canada.

Douglas & McIntyre Ltd.
1615 Venables Street
Vancouver, British Columbia

Canadian Cataloguing in Publication Data

Usmiani, Renate, 1931–
    Michel Tremblay
    (Studies in Canadian Literature; 15)

    Bibliography: p.
    ISBN 0-88894-304-0

    1. Tremblay, Michel, 1943-   —Criticism and
interpretation. I. Title. II. Series.
PS8539.R47Z88   C842'.54   C81-091282-1
PQ3919.2.T73Z88

Typesetting by The Typeworks, Mayne Island
Cover design by Nancy Legue
Printed and bound in Canada by D.W. Friesen & Sons Ltd.

For Tina and Sonia

Contents

CHAPTER ONE

From French-Canadian to
Québécois *Theatre*

Three widely divergent dates mark the "beginning" of theatre history in the French-speaking part of Canada. Depending on attitude and point of view, one can trace this history back as far as 1606, or see it originating as recently as 1948 or even 1968. The year 1606 is the date of the first theatrical ever to be produced in Nouvelle France, Marc Lescarbot's naval extravaganza *The Theatre of Neptune;* it marks the beginning of *French* theatre on the new continent. Nineteen forty-eight saw the premiere performance of Gratien Gélinas's *Ti-Coq*, which was considered the first genuinely *French-Canadian* play because in theme and language it reflected the reality of French Canada rather than that of the "mother country." Then, in 1968, a new era of aggressively *québécois* theatre began with the first performance of Michel Tremblay's *Les Belles-Soeurs*. Revolutionary in theme, language and technique, this play and those that followed set off a critical controversy which made Tremblay's work the most hotly debated issue on the Quebec cultural scene. For English-speaking Canadians, however, the debate remained largely theoretical, since the radical young author adamantly refused to grant English translation rights for his plays. This situation changed abruptly with the elections of 15 November 1976. After the Separatists' Parti Québécois under René Lévesque took power in the province of Quebec, an elated Michel Tremblay announced that he no longer felt bound to restrict his work to his French compatriots: "C'est pus ma job de refuser," adding the not altogether convincing explanation, "Depuis le 15 novembre, les Anglais et les Juifs sont devenus des minorités comme les autres. Ça m'enlève de toute façon un poids du coeur"[1] ("As of 15 November, the English and the Jews have become minorities like any others. It takes a weight off my mind, anyway"). One may have doubts regarding Tremblay's logic, especially in view of the fact that several of his plays had already been performed in English,[2] but there is certainly no question about the importance of his decision to finally make his work fully accessible to the English-speaking world.

Tremblay himself never anticipated the degree of success his work would achieve outside Quebec. His earlier complacency turned to dazed, if delighted, disbelief, punctuated with moments of downright panic, as translations appeared, productions multiplied and an ever-rising tide of critical accolades poured in from the North American continent as well as from Europe and beyond. Thirty-five-year-old Michel Tremblay, "le gars à la barbe sympathique,"[3] seemed to have realized one of the great dreams of Canadian dramatists: to "make it" on the international theatre scene. Tremblay's success must have come as something of a surprise to a number of his Quebec critics.

His work has, in fact, aroused greater critical controversy than that of any other Canadian dramatist—in or out of Quebec. With the performance of *Les Belles-Soeurs*, premiered at the Théâtre du Rideau Vert on 28 August 1968, it immediately became apparent that a bombshell had exploded on the cultural scene of Quebec and that the repercussions would be felt for a long time to come. Actually, the effect of the play was less that of a "bomb" than a display of theatrical fireworks, since Tremblay introduced to the Quebec stage not just one, but a number of revolutionary innovations. The most immediately obvious of these was the unashamed use of the Montreal working-class dialect, *joual*, liberally spiced with all the liturgical and scatological *sacres* (swear words) so dear to French Canadians. This departure from the accepted linguistic norms of the theatre would alone have sufficed to arouse a critical tempest; emotions ran high in both defence and denunciation of the *joual*. Beyond the level of language, Tremblay further challenged his audience by presenting them with a starkly naturalistic mirror image of themselves, a kind of *théâtre-vérité* which might make you cringe, but whose faithfulness to life you could not deny. And beyond the naturalism of the production, the audience was also confronted with recurring alienation techniques à la Brecht (choruses, characters "frozen" into monologues, etc.), clearly aimed at forcing a response: recognition, questioning, desire to change — in short, a raising of consciousness.

In spite of the obvious universal appeal of Tremblay's work, as proved by its eventual success on several continents, critical reaction in Quebec tended to take a narrow view. Critics either praised or condemned the work solely on the basis of its application to the social and cultural scene in Quebec. Not unexpectedly, criticism focussed on two major issues, Tremblay's use of *joual* and his particular brand of realism. For a while, the "joual crisis" set off by *Les Belles-Soeurs* overshadowed all other critical considerations.

The term itself, "joual," is simply a dialect version of the pronunciation of "cheval." Taken as a special idiom, it is defined by Lise Gauvin as a "langage-vérité . . . d'où l'on ne cherche pas à éliminer les anglicismes, les barbarismes et les Canadianismes"[4] ("a realistic language . . . which does not seek to eliminate anglicisms, barbarisms and Canadianisms").

The reaction to the appearance of *joual* on stage was immediate — and violent. Conservatives deplored its use, while radicals, interestingly enough, were split on the issue. To the conservative critics, the purists, the use of *joual* in literature, and particularly on the stage, represented a form of capitulation before the forces of mediocrity, vulgarity and cultural decline. As early as 1965, the year Tremblay wrote *Les Belles-Soeurs*, Yerri Kempf warned young writers against the perils of their new linguistic experiments: "l'usage d'une langue détériorée, au vocabulaire limité, à la syntaxe douteuse, empêche tout progrès social et voue la collectivité qui s'obstine à y recourir à la médiocrité"[5] ("the use of a corrupted language, with a limited vocabulary and a questionable syntax, prevents all social progress and condemns the community who persists in its use to mediocrity"). Many young radicals, on the other hand, hailed the use of *joual* as a major step through which *québécois* culture was finally asserting its independence from centuries-old bondage to the culture of France, the mother country, a partial liberation on the level of language which carried strong political overtones. "La libération au niveau de la parole révèle une libération globale, ou au moins une amorce de la désaliénation" ("Liberation on the level of language reveals liberation on all levels, or at least the beginning of disalienation"), wrote Jules Audet in 1966.[6] Other critics, though equally radical, have taken a totally different view of the use of *joual*. They see in it not an instrument of liberation but rather a symptom of defeat: a language whose very texture expresses the alienation, lack of identity, inability to communicate and tragic impotence of Quebec society. As such, it reflects a social reality which cannot be denied and so the artist must use it — as a necessary evil.

Tremblay himself, though well aware of the political implications of his choice of language, tends to shrug off the issue; his concern is with his characters, who must express themselves in such a way as to become believable and effective. As long as his characters move in a milieu where *joual* is the normal form of expression, they must necessarily speak *joual* — not the *joual* of the streets, of course, but a transposed form of that speech which will create the illusion of a realistic idiom on stage.

Tremblay's themes have aroused almost as much controversy as his use of *joual*. His starkly naturalistic descriptions of what passes for family life in the slums of East Montreal and his excursions into the lower depths of the Main (rue St. Laurent), with its cheap cabarets, drag bars and population of colourful riffraff, were enough to arouse the violent ire of many conservative citizens and critics. In 1972, for instance, *Les Belles-Soeurs* was considered too sordid a picture of Canadian manners to be shown to the outside world. The minister of cultural affairs refused it a subvention to follow up an invitation to play in Paris and sent instead Gélinas's innocuous *Yesterday the Children Were Dancing*, a play set in a most respectable milieu and written, moreover, in impeccable French. Professional and academic critics accused Tremblay of vulgarity, cynicism, distortion of reality; others, however, hailed him as the messiah of a new liberated theatre, free from the pious lies and false archetypes of traditional French-Canadian literature.

Jean-Claude Germain was the first to proclaim the new age ushered in by *Les Belles-Soeurs:* "ce théâtre québécois de libération qui vient de naître"[7] ("this *québécois* theatre of liberation which has just been born"); and he was followed by Michel Bélair, who sees in the work of Tremblay the first manifestation of a "new" *québécois* theatre, both realistic and revolutionary. Here, at last, was an author ready to assert the "real" identity of the Québécois — and even though the "cure d'identification"[8] might be painful, it was certain to be profitable and liberating. Tremblay's work was thus considered a genuine beginning, as opposed to the work of Gélinas and his fellow realists, who were accused of not having gone far enough in expressing the *québécois* identity and *québécois* concerns.[9]

Obviously, such an attitude takes too narrow a view of the importance of the theatrical tradition in French Canada from which the Tremblay opus evolved. Certainly *Les Belles-Soeurs* did not appear suddenly, ex nihilo. The tradition out of which it grew may be condemned, or rejected; it cannot be denied.

Love of theatre has always been a integral part of life in French Canada. After all, the "glorious" period of Nouvelle France coincided with the age of Louis XIV, the Sun King, at whose splendid court in Paris and Versailles the great masterpieces of Corneille, Racine and Molière were premiered. No wonder that the gentlemen of Nouvelle France were eager to emulate as best they could the glories of the mother country. The colony may not have boasted a printing press, but it had an active theatrical life ranging from occasional spectacles to performances of the French classics, often staged remarkably soon after their Paris or Versailles premiere. Corneille, whose *Le Cid* was produced in Quebec in 1646, was especially popular. Molière's *Tartuffe*, which had become a cause célèbre in France, also brought about a scandal in the New World, and its proposed performance was suppressed under somewhat unsavoury circumstances by the ecclesiastical authorities in 1694. Molière did not return to the Quebec stage until after the Conquest.

Throughout the eighteenth century, French theatre was

kept alive, oddly enough, by the British officers and administrators who manned the garrisons — a reflection of the general francophilia of the age which had spread from the old world to the new. However, among the French population itself, theatre went into a state of decline, especially after the war years and the Conquest, which proved economically disastrous and psychologically traumatic. *Survivance-résistance* was to be the central concern of the French in Canada from then on.

Even so, theatre did not die out altogether. Ironically, the lifeline that kept it afloat was provided by the Church — avowed enemy of all frivolity — through its educational institutions. The *collèges* and seminaries kept up a serious tradition of theatre, with regular performances of the classics along with the inevitable moral and didactic works which the good Fathers who ran these institutions felt duty-bound to produce for the benefit of their charges.

By the nineteenth century, a definite revival of interest in theatre had taken place. Aside from the *théâtres de collège*, whose intent was moral and educational, there now sprang up numerous amateur companies which brought back the sense of joyous entertainment that is the essence of the theatre. Although these companies had to contend with the severe objections unceasingly raised against their activities by the ecclesiastical leaders, as well as harassment from the political authorities who suspected them of revolutionary and subversive tendencies, they continued well into the twentieth century. Playwriting became a fashionable pastime. The results of this dramatic activity were less than perfect; however, the amateur companies did keep alive the traditions of performance and playgoing throughout these difficult years. They were encouraged in their efforts by the increasing number of professional touring companies who passed through Montreal and Quebec (the great Sarah Bernhardt visited Montreal no less than six times between 1880 and 1916). These tours gave the local population some idea of an international repertoire and professional standards of performance.

Professional standards did not apply to theatre in French Canada until well into the twentieth century. The transition from amateur production to professionalism took place grad-

ually, of course. It was attributable mainly to the achievements
of two groups who operated independently of each other: the
Compagnons, and the drama division of Radio-Canada. Although the contribution of these two groups laid the foundation
for a later *québécois* theatre, the attitudes underlying their work
differed so radically from the tenor and tone of later plays that
one can understand those who would like to sweep aside this
entire tradition.

The Compagnons started out in 1937 as a regular *théâtre de
collège*, at the Collège de St.-Laurent. Their director, Father
Emile Legault, had been sent to Europe by his superiors to
study the Christian revival movement in the theatre. When he
returned, he was able to build up a solid international reper-
tory of classical and modern plays, produced in a professional
manner, having poetic vision and using many of the modern
techniques of stylization. The Compagnons became instru-
mental in creating an interested and knowledgeable theatre
audience in Montreal. In addition, they became the first serious training centre for young actors and directors, many of
whom eventually started companies of their own. The orienta-
tion of this brand of theatre, originating with the Compagnons,
was very definitely towards the French classics.

The same can be said about the drama produced by
Radio-Canada, which from the start was extremely conscious
of its mission to bring the best in French and classical European
theatre to its audiences everywhere; a number of special educational series were devised for that very purpose.[10] However,
unlike live theatre in the forties and fifties, Radio-Canada also
made a special point of producing original plays—thus effectively turning radio drama into Canada's first and, for two dec-
ades at least, only national theatre. Although related chronologically, it was at the opposite pole philosophically from the
"théâtre québécois" which followed.

The radio plays written during the forties and fifties by
authors such as Yves Theriault, Yvette Naubert and Félix
Leclerc catapult the audience back into the spirit of the Middle
Ages. Frequent use of legend, fairy tale and parable; spontaneous and childlike integration of all the elements of Christian mythology (miracles, angels, saints) into the fabric of the

story; simple faith, orthodox morality, rural settings and idealized villagers all combine to create a sense of "once upon a
time," though the characters and the settings are firmly rooted
in the culture and folklore of rural Quebec.

Frequent lyricism and a highly poetic tone largely account
for the charm of many of these plays. Their anachronistic tone
corresponds to that of the *terroir* literature of Quebec, which
flourished from the middle of the nineteenth century until the
Second World War. *Terroir* poems and novels provided idyllic
interpretations of the "agriculturism" and "messianism" gospel
preached by the Church in its efforts to stave off the moral
dangers of urbanization.

It remained for Gratien Gélinas to acknowledge the fact
that French Canada, at the time of World War II, was no
longer an idyllically rural community, and to bring this realization before a theatre audience. The important breakthrough
here was not really *Ti-Coq*, the play which put the year 1948 on
the calendar of important events in the history of French-
Canadian theatre, but Gélinas's earlier and somewhat humbler
"paraliterary" creation: Fridolin, a character who first appeared
on the radio and, from 1938 to 1946, was the central figure in an
annual satirical revue. *Fridolinons*, as the revue was called,
achieved immediate success and played to packed houses night
after night at the large Monument National theatre.

As a genre, the satirical revue is free from many of the re-
straints of the more serious "legitimate" stage, and for this reason Gélinas was able to use Fridolin as an instrument to shatter
the traditional, pious myths of French-Canadian society. His
attacks were aimed at the very core of the moral value system — religion and the family — as well as at the many social and
political ills of his time. *Fridolinons*, then, set the tone for the
generation of "consciousness-raising" playwrights that was to
appear in the sixties. The revue was revolutionary in a number
of ways:

1. *The character of Fridolin.* A typical teenage boy from the
working-class district of Montreal, Fridolin — with his short
pants, hockey sweater and faithful slingshot — is the first repre-
sentative of the urban proletariat to appear on the French-

Canadian stage. In spite of the essentially realistic conception of the character and the episodes in which he figures, he also carries certain symbolic overtones which makes him immediately recognizable as the embodiment of French Canada itself. Poverty-stricken, rejected and long-suffering ("eh souffrance!" is his favourite expression), he nevertheless exhibits an unending ability to bounce back and try again after each disappointment, thus clearly demonstrating the *survivance-résistance* motto of his people. The slingshot he carries discreetly hints at the possibility that, like the young David, he may someday overcome Goliath.

2. *The setting.* Fridolin's universe is the same *fond de cour,* the colourful microcosm of city backyard and back alley, which we shall find as the setting of most of Tremblay's plays.

3. *The language.* Although not fully *joual,* the Fridolin sketches are written in a popular idiom, heavily interspersed with anglicisms, a language far removed from the elegance of classical French which had been considered de rigueur on stage until then.

4. *The themes.* The Fridolin sketches clearly reflect the economic nationalism of the period. There is a great deal of social satire as well as thinly veiled attacks against the political authorities. "Notre Maurice" (Duplessis) is the source of a good part of the fun.

Gélinas also uses his acid humour to demolish the traditional concepts of religion and the family by showing the realities beyond the pious façades. The tone of many of the sketches is definitely revolutionary, since the entire hierarchy of authority, from parents to God, is exposed as a fraud. Gélinas offers no solutions, but he does make a clear diagnosis of the underlying difficulty: "You see, God, the big failing of my people is that they have no confidence in themselves," one of his characters confides in the Almighty. It is this lack of confidence, this fear and timidity, that the later *québécois* theatre would attempt to exorcise.

In many ways, then, the Fridolin revues of Gélinas must be seen as a direct antecedent of the theatre of Michel Tremblay. Gélinas's reputation as a conservative writer, of course, is not based on the revues, which, like all cabaret-style entertainment, were ephemeral (the texts were not published until 1980), but on his contribution to the "legitimate" stage. In these terms, *Ti-Coq* does represent a beginning — characters and settings which the audience could identify as "bien de chez nous" — but ideologically the play does not move out of the value system propounded in the earlier *terroir* type of literature.

This "first French-Canadian play," in 1948, deals with the most common of postwar themes, the soldier who returns from war to find his girl married to another, and here Gélinas adheres fully to the traditional idealization of marriage and family as well as to the accepted respect for religion and the authority of the Church. The theme of conscription, the most burning political issue in French Canada throughout the war, is touched upon only lightly. Nevertheless, audiences immediately identified with *Ti-Coq*. The appeal of the play, above and beyond the sentimental value of the story line, undoubtedly lay in its realism, greatly enhanced by the use of a popular idiom. Audiences and critics also quickly seized upon the symbolic significance of the "bastard" motif used in the play. Ti-Coq is not only the little guy's Everyman; the fact of his illegitimate birth, which makes him an outsider and a second-class citizen, elevates him to symbolic significance, an embodiment of the alienation and lack of identity felt by the Québécois. Tremblay uses a similar, if more powerful, device to underline the marginality of French-Canadian society: the symbolism of the transvestite.

The realistic tradition which began with Gélinas continued throughout the fifties with the plays of Marcel Dubé. Dubé is not an innovator like Gélinas, nor is he a revolutionary like Tremblay. His contribution within the evolution of theatre in French Canada is consolidation rather than originality. As a writer for television more than the stage, his main goal is entertainment, which he pursues through psychological realism. In spite of all the accusations brought against Dubé for not going far enough in either realism of language or depth of social analysis, one can find in the best of his many works an often astute treatment of all those themes which mark the new *québécois* theatre of the Tremblay generation. One of the songs in *Un Simple Soldat* provides the leitmotif for the entire dramatic work of Dubé:

La vie est morne et sans couleur
Et sans espoir dans la rue sans nom. . . .

(Act 3, scene 12)

(Life is dull and colourless
and without hope on a nameless street. . . .)

These two lines sum up perfectly the underlying tone of despair and hopelessness that is characteristic of modern literature generally, and the particular form that these attitudes take in a *québécois* context. It is the same "maudite vie plate" ("this goddamn senseless life") motif which Tremblay uses as the theme of the central ode in *Les Belles-Soeurs.* This sense of hopelessness provides the psychological and social background for most of Dubé's plays. The teen-agers of *Zone* who set up a smuggling operation, ending in the death of their chief, Tarzan, risk their lives rather than face the *maudite vie plate* which, to them, is the very essence of adult life; the wealthy couples of *Les Beaux Dimanches* and *Bilan* float their weekends away on a sea of scotch and, between flirtations and tranquillizers, desperately fight off the realization of the meaninglessness of their lives.

To this basic theme, Dubé adds a number of concerns central to *québécois* culture. The theme of alienation is taken up in *Un Simple Soldat* with the character of Joseph Latour, who, unable to find meaningful employment at home, eventually dies a hero having fought in two foreign wars, first for "les Anglais" in Europe and then for the Americans in Korea. Dubé also portrays the traditional lack of self-confidence of French Canadians, which he diagnoses as the result of centuries-long indoctrination by church and state. In *Florence*, the central character eventually breaks loose from this atmosphere of confinement and makes her escape, somewhat naively, by moving to New York. Perhaps the most striking aspect of the work of Dubé, however, is his condemnation of the family and his negative view of love. It was Dubé who dared to describe Quebec as "le pays des mal aimés" ("the land of those who are loved badly," or better, "of those who do not know how to love").[11] And although it remained for Tremblay to expose the full horror of self-destructive family life in a working-class setting, Dubé's affluent bourgeois families provide a rather good illustration of the same idea. From 1951 on, then, and continuing through the sixties into the seventies, Marcel Dubé established a solid tradition of realistic playwriting, thus providing first a basis for and later an accompaniment to the work of Michel Tremblay.

Tremblay himself is to a large extent the product of the two major social forces that exercised their influence on the formative years of many young writers of his generation: television and the Quiet Revolution. He was ten years old when television came to Montreal in 1952 and, like most of his contemporaries, he was hooked. When he began to write at the age of twelve, his characters were taken from the popular "Famille Plouffe" series, and not long afterwards he tried to follow the style of García Lorca, whose work he had seen produced on television. It is certainly not coincidental that the "new *québécois* theatre" had its beginning in the television generation.

More important from the ideological, if not the technical, point of view was the fact of the Quiet Revolution. With the death of Maurice Duplessis in 1959, all the social and cultural ferment which had been repressed for so long finally came to the surface. There followed a wave of far-reaching, often radical reforms that changed the face of Quebec society, as Vatican II had changed every aspect of Catholicism. First and foremost, a sense of hope emerged. Paul Sauvé, who held power for the three months immediately following the death of Duplessis, coined the motto "désormais" ("henceforth"), which expressed the possibility of better things to come. Under the influence of pressure groups centred at the social sciences faculty of the Université Laval, the government began to introduce reforms aimed at modernizing the educational system, as well as a number of much-needed social and economic changes.

On the cultural scene, what the Quiet Revolution achieved, principally, was a clearing of the air. For the intellectuals, artists and writers of French Canada, it had now become possible to undertake a wide-reaching *prise de conscience*, a search into the collective self. They were free to diagnose the ills affecting the community and to offer remedies. The radical review *Parti Pris*, founded in 1963 (the year of the Front de

Libération du Québec [FLQ] violence), summed up these ills as alienation on the political, economic and cultural levels. The task of the theatre thus became to denounce the past and to liberate — as well as create — a sense of identity. In an address to the arts faculty of the Université de Montréal, Claude Jasmin strongly denied the traditional assumption that Quebec already had developed an autonomous literature and he brushed aside past achievements as nothing more than a few "attempts" of little significance.[12] Because of its supposed colonial tendency to lean heavily on French influences, all this earlier literature retained the designation French-Canadian; the new literature from the mid-sixties on was termed "québécois."

This new *québécois* theatre to which Tremblay belongs branched out in a number of directions during the sixties. The psychological realism of Gratien Gélinas continued with the work of Dubé, Loranger and others. A strongly experimental stream developed among the very young, as the modern techniques of continental Europe became better known in Montreal (Brecht, Dario Fo and the Theatre of the Absurd were especially important influences). The mainstream of theatrical writing during this period, however, was political, with very little concern for universal values or "bourgeois aestheticism." Political plays ranged from the outright call to violence of Jacques Ferron's ironic *La Tête du roi* (1963), to Gélinas's highly civilized treatment of the Separatist issue in a more general context, the conflict of generations in *Yesterday the Children Were Dancing*. The sixties was a period of fermentation of ideas, experimentation and dynamism on the theatre scene. Its many and divergent elements eventually found a solid synthesis in the work of Michel Tremblay.

CHAPTER TWO

Contexts of the Tremblay Opus

"But where shall I begin my accusation? How to end it? What to put in the middle?"—these lines, from the *Electra* of Euripides, chosen by Tremblay as a motto for his monologue novel, *C't'à ton tour, Laura Cadieux* (*It's Your Turn, Laura Cadieux*), could well serve as a heading for his entire opus, in which the "accusation" shifts from social to political to metaphysical, depending on the particular emphasis of particular works. When Tremblay wrote *Les Belles-Soeurs* in 1965, *québécois* theatre was eminently ready for just such a strong voice.

That same year, the magazine *La Barre du jour* brought out a special drama issue[1] to underline the urgent need for a renewal in the theatre. "We believe the theatre to be a school for collective liberation," stated the editorial, "an essential factor of disalienation." Individual articles also emphasized the revolutionary and consciousness-raising aspect of the theatre-about-to-come and its expected role in the definition of a *québécois* identity. It is ironic to contemplate that, when this new type of theatre did appear, it was not recognized: *Les Belles-Soeurs* was not produced until 1968. Partly because of his revolutionary use of *joual*, partly because of the complexity of Tremblay's themes, so different from the conventional theatre of the sixties, the importance of his contribution was not immediately apparent.

The two major theatrical events of 1968—aside from the history-making production of *Les Belles-Soeurs*—were Robert

Gurik's adaptation of *Hamlet*, and Françoise Loranger's *Le Chemin du Roy*, two perfect examples of technically ingenious but intellectually uncomplicated political theatre. In *Hamlet, Prince du Québec*, Gurik turns the Shakespearian tragedy into an allegory of contemporary Quebec, in which Hamlet (Quebec), oppressed by the King (Anglophone power) and Queen (the Church), with the aid of Horatio (René Lévesque) follows the dictates of the Ghost (de Gaulle, symbol of France), and eventually dies with the general's now famous "vive le Québec libre!" on his lips. Loranger's *Le Chemin du Roy* also takes its inspiration from de Gaulle's 1967 visit to Quebec; it is an attempt to capture the impact of that visit on the people.

Tremblay's theatre transcends any such narrow approach. From the beginning, he managed to achieve a double synthesis: a synthesis of the major theatrical traditions which, at least potentially, come together in contemporary French Canada, and a synthesis between universality and solid regionalism.

A young playwright working in Montreal in the sixties could not but be aware of three totally distinct theatrical traditions: the local tradition of realistic theatre developed by Gélinas and Dubé; the tradition of the American theatre, too close to home to be ignored; and the classical and modern European tradition, rejected by the more radical groups, but present nonetheless as a matrix and source of archetypes. While other dramatists felt compelled to make a choice between traditions, Tremblay instinctively took the path of synthesis, taking from each what it could contribute towards the aesthetic completeness of his own work.

Within the creative process, of course, the fusion of elements occurs on the level of the unconscious. Nevertheless, Tremblay is very much aware of the importance, to his work, of those he calls his "maîtres à penser." The themes, settings, characters and language of his plays clearly demonstrate his concern for the "regional" — in the sense of a realistic, slice-of-life — representation. He is also very much aware of the close ties between French-Canadian and American culture, stressing that the identity of the French Canadian does not depend upon a rejection of the American element in his life, but rather on a fully conscious acceptance of that fact. "We are not French but we are Québécois living in North America,"[2] he says, reflecting the attitudes of Jacques Languirand's then revolutionary article, "Le Québec et l'américanité."[3] Of American writers, the work of Tennessee Williams has been an especially important factor in Tremblay's artistic growth; one can also detect certain similarities with Edward Albee. Unlike many of his contemporaries, he does not feel compelled to cut himself off from the classical European tradition, or even that of France, in an attempt to flaunt his anticolonialism. On the contrary: as a schoolboy, Michel, who did not attend the *cours classique*, but had a friend who did, avidly read all the classical works he could borrow. He has always retained an enormous admiration for the formal perfection of Greek tragedy, especially the choral tragedies of Aeschylus. Without this classical background, he would never have been able to achieve the complex musical structures, largely based on choral techniques, which constitute the major artistic merit of his plays. As for the French classics, in one of his early works, *La Cité dans l'oeuf*, he went so far as to try to emulate Racine by restricting himself to a list of one hundred adjectives in an effort to achieve the simplicity of the neoclassical style. Of the more recent European playwrights, Beckett is his favourite. Although Tremblay's essential naturalism is far from the abstract style of Beckett, one can see in even these naturalistic plays a level where the imagery assumes a symbolic character not unlike that found in absurdist drama.

The second, and more important, synthesis achieved by Tremblay is the blending of universality and "québécitude." He himself feels very strongly that there is no contradiction between these terms; on the contrary, the more a writer is rooted in the realities of his own time and place, the more universal he may become. However, the universality of Tremblay's themes has not always been recognized by Quebec critics, who tend to gauge his work only in terms of the local and contemporary context, and to emphasize its "political" significance. In fact, the multiple levels on which his plays operate can be simplified into three basic categories: the story or anecdotal level (and on this level almost all of his work is regional/naturalistic); the socio-political level (which is present, in varying degrees, in all of his naturalistic plays and is strongly rooted in the problems of contemporary Quebec); and a universal/mythological level.

It is interesting to observe how closely such a three-level interpretation of Tremblay's work corresponds to Dante's directions regarding a proper reading of his *Divine Comedy*, which reflect the general medieval/patristic system of literary interpretation. Writing to his patron Can Grande della Scala, Dante pointed out that his work could be taken "literally," "morally" and "allegorically" — which, in twentieth-century terms, could be interpreted in a way that applies also to Tremblay: "literal" = basic anecdote; "moral" = socio-political message; "allegorical" = universal significance. The parallel is suggestive. It indicates a basic spiritual affinity, for, as we shall see, the medieval Florentine's concern for salvation is not as far removed as one would think at first glance from the naturalistic plays of the contemporary Québécois, which are also permeated with a basic mysticism and desire for transcendence.

The settings of Tremblay's plays also reflect this division into threefold levels of meaning. If we survey his opus from a topological point of view, we find a universe consisting of three distinct spheres, at decreasing levels of naturalism, which together form the basis for a mythology in the making.

1. Rue Fabre: daily life, the family

The street on which he grew up, the people on that street and, in particular, the noisy, crowded quarters where he was forced to spend his childhood left an indelible impression on Michel Tremblay. Rue Fabre to him is not just a street: it is a way of life. By his own admission, he cannot conceive of everyday life in any other setting than this, a tawdry "street without men," as he sees it. Of course, he does not see it realistically. His poetic vision centres on only one aspect of reality.

Tree-lined rue Fabre, in northeast Montreal, impresses the visitor as a typical lower-middle-class neighbourhood, not without a certain charm, with its outside staircases, balconies and postage-stamp size front lawns. Tremblay, however, focusses on the promiscuity of life along the back alley, with its filth and stench, peopled by colourful, but desperate characters. This is the world of *Les Belles-Soeurs*, the world of Marie-Louise and Léopold in *A toi, pour toujours, ta Marie Lou*, the palpable background to the telephone conversation of the three gossips in *Surprise! Surprise!*

Rue Fabre and the *maudite vie plate* motif go together in all the plays of this cycle, including the autobiographical *Bonjour, là, bonjour* and *En pièces détachées*. As a source of poetic inspiration, the street achieves its ultimate potential in Tremblay's most recent play, *Damnée Manon, Sacrée Sandra*, in which we find Sandra, the transvestite prostitute, and Manon, the old maid religious fanatic, pursuing their individual obsessions next door to each other. Rue Fabre also provides the background for the cycle of novels starting with *La Grosse Femme d'à côté est enceinte* (1978). The entire series will be highly autobiographical, with the author himself the child to be born from "la grosse femme."

2. THE MAIN: NIGHTLIFE, PROSTITUTION, HOMOSEXUALITY

This is a world of false glitter and real pathos: the world of *La Duchesse de Langeais,* of *Hosanna*, of Berthe, Carlotta and Gloria Star in *Trois Petits Tours;* a world of no exit where the only escape possible comes through illusion; where illusion is quickly shattered, as in *Demain matin, Montréal m'attend,* and heroism is stamped out, as in *Sainte Carmen de la Main*. In his program notes to *Sainte Carmen de la Main,* André Brassard has tried to explain the fascination of this particular street (actually, boulevard St. Laurent):

La Main, pour Tremblay, pour moi, pour les personnages de la dramaturgie de Tremblay, c'est le Paradis. . . . La Main, c'est le royaume des marginaux, des homosexuels, des lesbiennes, des prostituées, des travestis. C'est là où ils se retrouvent et peuvent se créer un milieu plus confortable que le milieu dit «normal» . . . la Main, c'est la Terre Promise: une terre où on peut être «comme les autres,» ou «pas comme les autres»: aucune importance. Inutile de dire que je me réfère à la rue St. Laurent d'avant l'enquête sur la moralité du maire Drapeau. . . . La Main, c'est un quartier plein de maisons de prostitution, de maisons de jeu, de cabarets, de lumière, de bruit! . . . c'est aussi . . . toute la partie defavorisée, oubliée du prolétariat, ces gens qui s'offrent en «cheap labor,» qui ne survivent qu'en se vendant, et en se vendant mal. La sous-classe de la société.[4] (The Main, for Tremblay, for myself, for the characters of Tremblay's dramaturgy, represents Paradise. . . . The Main is the kingdom of the marginals, the homosexuals, the lesbians, the prostitutes, the transvestites. They can meet each other there and create for themselves a milieu which is more comfortable than the "normal" one . . . the Main means the Promised Land: a land where one may be "like the others," or "not like the others," and it doesn't matter. Needless to say, I speak of the rue St. Laurent before the inquest into morality by Mayor Drapeau. . . . The Main is a part of town full of houses of prostitution, gambling places, cabarets, lights and noise! . . . it is also . . . the underprivileged and forgotten part of the proletariat, those who offer themselves for sale cheap, who can survive only by selling themselves, and sell themselves poorly. The underlayer of society.)

It is not impossible to cross over from the world of rue Fabre to that of the Main, and several of Tremblay's characters have made the transition — most notably, Carmen (from the household of Léopold and Marie-Louise in *A toi, pour toujours, ta Marie-Lou* to the Rodeo café in *Sainte Carmen de la Main*). Sandra the transvestite takes the opposite route when he/she eventually returns to the street of his/her childhood. For the women who are caught in the emotional and physical trap of frustration that the family constitutes within the limitations of an inbred neighbourhood, the Main stands for glamour, freedom, life itself. However, seen within its own context, the world of the Main turns out to be ultimately as inbred, frustrating and limiting, in its own kinky way, as the petty household world around rue Fabre. The desire to escape towards something better, a greater, more fulfilling type of life, is felt just as strongly by the nightclub artists and male and female prostitutes as it is by the rosary-reciting *belles-soeurs*. All the glory of the Main is but illusion, its inhabitants eventually are forced to realize, as the author uncovers layer after layer of self-deception — for example, when he shows us the grand old Duchesse de Langeais, the high-flying courtesan who has "fucked on four continents," crying over the facts of his/her life as they stare him/her in the face from the bottom of a now empty bottle of scotch.

While the people of the rue Fabre escape into dreams of the Main, and the people of the Main into dreams of glory and fame, the author of both of these worlds has created a private escape for himself—the third and least realistic sphere of his universe, a world of fantasy and transcendence.

3. THE GREAT BEYOND ("LE GRAND AILLEURS"): GODS, SINNERS AND FANTASIES

Tremblay's novel of pure fantasy, *La Cité dans l'oeuf,* came out in 1968, the same year as *Les Belles-Soeurs*—a fact that illustrates perfectly the dual aspect of his opus: naturalism and fantasy, materialism and spiritualism, immanence and transcendence. Other works of fantasy include a collection of short stories, *Contes pour buveurs attardés,* and the plays *Les Paons* and *Les Socles.*[5] As opposed to the stark naturalism of the two worlds described earlier, Tremblay's fantasy world is a place of dreams, where the laws of time and space are suspended. It is, nevertheless, a self-contained universe having certain recognizable and recurring features: the mysterious land of Paganka, starting point of the journey towards the Great Beyond; idols who come to life; fallen gods, and men who achieve divine status through the initiation ritual of crime. The underlying theme of the fantasies is a desire to break through the barrier of immanence into a state of transcendence; however, all such attempts end in tragic frustration.

This brief survey clearly illustrates the enormous diversity of the Tremblay opus. In genre, it extends to drama, novel and short story; in theme, to everyday and family life, to the life of the outcasts of society, to dream, fantasy and nightmare; in technique, it ranges from naturalism to the use of every stylization device known to modern theatre, and leans heavily on classical models as well. There is diversity even in language, for in spite of the fact that Tremblay has become known as the pioneer of *joual* on stage, he has also used pure "classical" French (in all the works based on fantasy). In spite of this wide spectrum, the dramatic opus as a whole shows an underlying unity, with each individual play contributing another facet in a mosaic-like construction.

On the literal level, the three spheres (rue Fabre, the Main, the Great Beyond) have little in common: each one forms a perfect unity in itself. Tremblay has been attacked for using the same characters and settings in the various plays that make up each of his "worlds." The criticism is totally unjustified because it fails to recognize the mythopoeic intention of the author, which is less to create individual, self-contained "plots" than to produce a mosaic or epic of his people. The mythologizing intent is obvious as we follow the same characters, in the same basic setting, through play after play. Numerous other writers have used similar techniques; a familiar example is Faulkner's Yoknapatawpha County. Tremblay himself has explained his intentions: "I decided to take up these characters again because I needed them, because, very simply, I thought they were good characters. Later, I decided I wanted to create a kind of large epic, which takes place in one particular street, at one particular point in the history of Quebec, and to make out of it a microcosm. . . . "[6]

If we examine the plays on the "moral" level of sociopolitical allegory, the overall unity of the work becomes much more apparent. Although primarily concerned with aesthetic considerations, Tremblay is enough of a Brechtian to reject any purely "culinary" type of theatre: "J'veux pas faire passer de bonnes soirées au monde. . . . J'veux qu'ils réagissent, en ayant peur, en braillant, en riant, en se disant 'Il faut q'ça change'"[7] ("I don't want to give people a pleasant evening at the theatre. . . . I want them to react, to be afraid, to cry, to laugh, to tell themselves 'This has got to change'"). His avowed purpose is to use the theatre as a "sociological instrument." In the rue Fabre cycle of plays, he does this mainly by exposing the ugly realities behind traditional myths and façades and by forcing the audience to recognize the truth of facts and situations which they would prefer to ignore. The shock of recognition produced by such plays as *Les Belles-Soeurs* should logically lead to a heightening of consciousness (Brecht's "this has got to change'") and, possibly, to action. Some of the plays convey a message directly, through the symbolism inherent in the characters or situations. Thus, the parents in *A toi, pour toujours, ta Marie-Lou* represent Quebec in the past, their joint suicide the only way out; the pious sister, Manon, who refuses to move out of her parents' house after their death and continues to live in her mother's tradition of self-imposed martyrdom, is Quebec in the present (early seventies), while Carmen, the sister who breaks away to become a Western singer at a Main café, stands for the future.

The Main cycle of plays complements the message of the domestic tragedies. The setting itself, and the choice of this particular milieu, is a plea for marginality, for freedom of the individual from the pressures of society, as well as for the freedom of marginal societies, such as the French-Canadian community on the North American continent. As with the rue Fabre plays, we also find a plea for sexual liberation—and, as in all modern literature, sexual liberation also signifies liberation generally, of the individual as well as the community. Tremblay comes close to Tennessee Williams in this respect— Williams also tends to transpose social situations onto a sexual plane. As for the prevalence of transvestite characters in his work, these can be seen as inverted and caricatured versions of the sex symbol, a central element in the consumer society much hated by Tremblay. They also carry heavy overtones of political symbolism: the transvestite par excellence represents loss of identity, as well as impotence. The author himself insists on the parallel: "On est un peuple qui s'est déguisé pendant des années pour ressembler à un autre peuple. C'est pas des farces! On a été travestis pendant 300 ans"[8] ("We are a people who have disguised ourselves for years to resemble another people. It's no joke! We have been transvestites for 300 years").

Thus we see that all the basically realistic plays of Tremblay share the same socio-political intent: to destroy the conscious and unconscious taboos of his society and bring about a liberation on the level of the individual as well as the community. We find no such clearly spelled out message in his fantasy world, though the flight into fantasy is, in itself, one more illustration of the awareness, common to all his "realistic" characters, that life, such as it is, is not acceptable. On the universal/mythological level, all of his work comes together in a total unity of spirit.

Tremblay considers himself something of a mystic. This may come as a surprise to the casual reader. However, if we accept Ben-Ami Scharfstein's definition of mysticism as "a name for our infinite appetites,"⁹ the term can apply equally well to every part of the Tremblay universe. The most general underlying theme of all his works is the universal desire of the human being to transcend his finite condition. It is the same elementary drive of the spirit that animates the archetypal Doctor Faustus. As with Faustus, Tremblay's search for the absolute, for the Ultimate Experience, takes him through realms of sensuality as well as into the world of spirits. A statement made by the narrator of one of his short stories might well serve as a description of the author's own perception of his life: "Mais je ne suis pas né pour mener une vie de bourgeois. Je suis né pour parcourir le temps et l'espace, pour remonter le fleuve de la vie vers sa source . . . "¹⁰ ("But I was not born to lead a bourgeois life. I was born to travel through time and space, to go up to the springs of the river of life . . . ").

In the face of plays as starkly materialistic as *Les Belles-Soeurs* or *A toi, pour toujours, ta Marie-Lou,* such a mystical approach to the works may seem inappropriate. There is, of course, a basic difference in the manner in which the *soif d'absolu,* the desire for transcendence, manifests itself in the more realistically conceived characters as opposed to the characters of the fantasies. Whereas the realistic characters are only dimly aware of any such need within them — their need is largely unconscious — the characters of the fantasy world are fully conscious of their metaphysical desires and set out methodically to escape from the barriers of finite life.

With the characters of the rue Fabre, the element of the spiritual is so palpably absent that it becomes, in fact, a presence. Watching the fifteen women of *Les Belles-Soeurs* as they reveal sordid detail upon sordid detail, the pettiness, prejudices and claustrophobic narrowness of their everyday lives, one is tempted to cry out, like Tolstoy's Akim in *The Power of Darkness*, "You have no soul!" Although Germaine and her sisters would never be able to formulate the source of their profound dissatisfaction and frustration quite this way, they are at least conscious of a very basic lack in their lives. That this lack is not a material one becomes apparent in the *maudite vie plate* ode, leitmotif of the play. The rebellion against life that these women feel has nothing to do with poverty — there is, after all, food to be cooked, clothing to be washed, shopping to be done. Germaine Lauzon would be hard put to define exactly why she curses her life with such vehemence; she is aware only of the fact that it does not give her the kind of fulfilment she would have liked. By forcing upon the audience an almost unbearably vulgar accumulation of materialistic detail, on the one hand, and by reinforcing the impression with various stylization techniques on the other, Tremblay makes us painfully aware of the missing dimension in the lives of his characters. "Maudite vie plate" does not only mean daily drudgery and a less than affluent lifestyle; first and foremost, it means emotional and spiritual starvation. On a more tangible, physical level, this starvation corresponds to the sexual frustration which is a permanent feature of life in this particular milieu.

Moving to the Main, we find that the characters achieve a somewhat higher level of awareness: they have, after all, broken out of the original prison of family life. Yet in moments of lucidity they realize the tawdriness of their existence; they, too, are filled with a dimly understood need to escape into another world which they suspect must exist somewhere beyond the Main. Instead of rebelling against the *maudite vie plate*, however, they manifest their dissatisfaction in dreams of glory and greatness; in other words, they take refuge from reality in a fantasy world of daydream and illusion. Thus, Berthe, the middle-aged spinster who spends her life in the ticket booth of the Coconut Inn cabaret (*Trois Petits Tours*), dreams of the great actress she might have been. Claude, become Hosanna the transvestite, sees him/herself as the best ever impersonator of Elizabeth Taylor playing Cleopatra—a truly dizzying spin of role playing. The Duchesse de Langeais over her bottle of scotch tries to convince both her audience and herself that she is looking back over the most successful career ever achieved by a male courtesan. Of all the characters of the Main, only one, Carmen, achieves the ultimate in human experience: understanding and love. It is with good reason, therefore, that she becomes "Sainte" Carmen, saint and martyr in every sense of these words, including the Christian. Of Carmen, it could truly be said that she has found her "soul." She understands the needs of others and her duty towards them as an artist. When she tries to put her newly gained understanding into practice, she is instantly put to death by the forces of the Establishment, personified by Maurice, king of the Main. She thus becomes a true Saviour figure, and the play a universal, and desperately pessimistic, parable about art, life and salvation.

The supernatural element, only implied in the more realistic works, becomes the dominant factor in the fantasies. The narrator of *La Cité dans l'oeuf* consciously attempts to force his way into the world of the Great Beyond. When he succeeds, he discovers that in order to restore the fallen gods, save the universe and achieve ultimate power for himself, he must break through the barrier of crime: he must kill. The same theme appears in the play *Les Paons*, which also reiterates the *eritis sicut deus* theme of the Genesis story: for the man and the woman of this play, the ritual of admission to immortality and godlike status — in other words, of entrance to the Great Beyond — demands the sacrificial murder of their children. In Tremblay's metaphysical universe, godliness does not mean happiness, however. Although immortal, his gods are often fallen divinities who expiate their crimes for all eternity. The answer to the quest for transcendence certainly does not lie in the attainment of such an Other World: Tremblay's essential pessimism comes through just as strongly here as in the more realistic works.

For a satisfactory solution to the meaning of mysticism in the work of Michel Tremblay, we must look to the last play of the cycle, *Damnée Manon, Sacrée Sandra*. It is here that all his themes finally converge. We are shown two possible escape routes from the *maudite vie plate*, curse of mankind: Sandra the transvestite has chosen the way of sexuality, Manon the prude that of religious mysticism. However, it soon turns out that Sandra's pursuits are as mystical as those of Manon, while Manon's religious fervours carry heavily sexual overtones. The message comes through loud and clear: sexual and religious experience are both forms of devotion which manifest in slightly different ways the same basic desire for mystical experience and its ultimate achievement, ecstasy.

The surprise ending of the play reinforces this point. Transported to another level of reality, we discover what we should have guessed all along, that both Sandra and Manon have been "invented" by Tremblay. In other words, the two characters are but physical incarnations, exteriorizations, of the two paths towards ecstasy conceived by the author. All along, it has been clear that Sandra and Manon really represent two complementary aspects of one overall personality. On that level, the world they inhabit, face to face, is not a physical reality on the rue Fabre, but the psychological reality of the poet's own mind.

The ultimate escape, then, comes back to the self: there is no other. The final realization that there is no transcendence beyond that which the self can provide constitutes the real tragedy in the work of Michel Tremblay. It is not the tragedy of the frustrated housewife, or the aging cabaret artist, though these may be real enough: it is the universal tragedy of man's passionate desire for an absolute, and the impossibility of satisfying this desire. Expressed in a variety of modes, styles and idioms, this realization remains the basic unifying idea that permeates the entire Tremblay opus.

To conclude the discussion of Tremblay's dramatic opus, a word about the problem of translation is in order. The success of the English versions of his plays suggests that the translations which have been produced so far are at least adequate. However, a close textual comparison between the French and English versions reveals a number of weaknesses.[11] For the most part, these are cultural as much as linguistic weaknesses and are therefore difficult to avoid.

The most important overall problem with any translation from Tremblay's *joual* into English is the inescapable loss of flavour in the description of the milieu, as well as a considerable weakening of the characters, whose picturesque qualities are based, as we have seen, on the author's imaginative use of his idiom. In the English versions, the characters come through, but nuances are absent and there is sometimes a considerable loss of pathos and colouration.

Since the major difficulties of translation remain fairly constant from play to play, I shall analyze them by means of two examples only, *La Duchesse de Langeais* and *Hosanna*. Both English versions are basically adequate renditions of the French originals. Close analysis, however, reveals a number of inadequacies in capturing character and milieu, inadequacies which can be summed up in five main points:

1. The wide range of French *sacres* must of necessity be rendered in the considerably more restricted vocabulary provided by the English language. In the process, the word "shit" emerges with alarming frequency in the English version, since this seems to be the favoured equivalent for a wide variety of French expressions. In general, scatology in English takes the place of religious and/or sexual terms in French. Here are a few examples of *sacres* in translation: in *La Duchesse de Langeais*, we find "I don't give a shit" ("je m'en crisse"); "shitty little worm" ("calice de profiteur"); "happy as pigs in shit" ("elles jouiraient comme des cochonnes"); in *Hosanna*, "Shit! I've broken a nail. That's the second one tonight! Shit!" ("Ciboé, j'me sus cassé un ongle. Verrat de bâtard, c'est le deuxième à soir!"). The range of the translations is definitely limited compared to the original versions!

2. English expressions used in the original French text serve to give certain ideas a special significance. There is no way to render this type of emphasis in a text that is English throughout. Thus, when the Duchesse speaks of her professional "standing," discusses her German "playboy" or casually mentions, "J'en ai vu de toutes les couleurs, pis de toutes les *size*, if you know what I mean," we are immediately conscious of the cosmopolitan aura with which she likes to surround herself. A translation cannot do justice to the bilingualism of the original text, any more than, to give an example from *Hosanna*, "a Cleopatra of the streets" can fully render Tremblay's "Elisabeth Taylor dans «Cléopâtre», en infiniment plus cheap." Hosanna's "the show must go on . . . and on . . . and on" becomes enormously pathetic just because the character is using a formula borrowed from a foreign language; the nuance is lost in translation.

To counteract the loss of the bilingual element, the translators occasionally insert French expressions into the English text. This is done to particular advantage in *La Duchesse de Langeais* ("garçon"; "oui, monsieur"; "vous savez," etc.). The technique is quite effective, but does not completely solve the problem.

3. Puns are by their very nature untranslatable, and this creates a serious loss in the English texts.

4. Essential nuances of character or feeling are sometimes lost through inaccurate translations. Thus, when the Duchesse complains, with a great deal of reserve, about her lukewarm whisky, "ce n'est pas bien, bien, bien bon," and the phrase is translated as "it tastes like shit," we have a definite vulgarization and distortion of the original. Similarly, when she refers to her poet lover as "pauv'p'tit garçon, va!" the phrase contains an element of maternal love and kindness which is totally lost in the no-nonsense "hopeless!" of the English version. Examples could be multiplied, of course.

5. English translations tend to be somewhat conservative in their rendering of sexual expressions. Phrases that might be reacted to with excessive shock are often watered down in more socially acceptable, but considerably less picturesque terms.

In spite of these weaknesses, the English renditions of the plays remain eminently readable. They also convey an adequate if by no means perfect idea of the original versions.

Tremblay himself is fully aware of the cultural as well as linguistic difficulties inherent in translation, since he has produced a number of translations and adaptations of plays by various authors, especially American. He deplores the custom of bringing to Quebec American plays translated into French by experts in Paris:

C'est pas assez niaiseux de prendre un texte américain, d'y faire traverser l'Atlantique, d'le faire maganer par des Français qui ne le comprennent pas à moitié, pis de le ramener ici. Franchement. Y commence à être temps qu'le monde se réveille, pis qu'y réalise qu'au Québec on est peut-être les seuls à pouvoir comprendre pis à pouvoir traduire du théâtre américain . . . nous autres, on est dedans, on en fait partie; on est des Américains.[12] (If it isn't idiotic to take an American text across the Atlantic, to have it ruined by Frenchmen who don't understand half of it, then to bring it back here. Honestly. It's about time for people to wake up, and to realize that in Quebec we are maybe the only ones who can understand and translate American theatre . . . we are right in there, we are part of it; we're Americans.)

Putting this theory into practice, Tremblay has translated four of Tennessee Williams's one-act plays under the collective title *Au pays du dragon,* as well as two plays by Paul Zindel, whose work bears a striking similarity in tone to Tremblay's own: *L'Effet des rayons gamma sur les vieux-garçons* (*The Effect of Gamma Rays on Man-in-the-Moon Marigolds*) and *Et Mademoiselle Roberge boit un peu* (*And Miss Reardon Drinks a Little*).

Whereas the plays chosen for translation obviously correspond to Tremblay's own literary preferences, his two adaptations were commissioned: Aristophanes' *Lysistrata* for the National Arts Centre, Ottawa, in 1969, and Dario Fo's contemporary, political version of an old Italian mystery cycle, *mistero buffo,* for the Théâtre du Nouveau Monde in 1973. Tremblay's interpretation of *Lysistrata* merits some attention. While following the basic plot outline of Aristophanes, he has made a number of essential changes which reflect the fundamental pessimism of the modern era. Most important, in the Tremblay version the restoration of peace as a result of the women's machinations is but an illusion; for "there will always be war." A surrealistic finale suggests the absurdity of any hope for peace: a "totally ridiculous" personification of Peace descends from heaven and dominates the stage, her white robe functioning as a screen for the projections of scenes of horror and violence, while the chorus repeats its threefold finale, "Car la guerre ne finira jamais" ("For war will never end"). Other changes include a demand by the women for permanent supremacy, which, like their attempt to win peace, is defeated by the men; greater realism, with the introduction of certain characters not found in Aristophanes (Lysistrata's husband, for instance); and the treatment of the choruses in Brechtian ballad style. The "essential Tremblay" is thus fully manifest even in those of his works which are not original but translation-adaptations—more testimony to the unity and originality of his considerable opus.

CHAPTER THREE

A Symphony of Frustrations: Les Belles-Soeurs

When *Les Belles-Soeurs* opened at the Théâtre du Rideau Vert on 28 August 1968, the event was hailed by the more radical element among Quebec critics as the dawn of a new era of liberation, both political and aesthetic. Written in 1965 and submitted to the selection committee of the 1967 Dominion Drama Festival, *Les Belles-Soeurs* was rejected by all but one member of the committee. Going over the head of a discouraged Tremblay, André Brassard organized a public reading of the manuscript at the Centre d'Essai des Auteurs Dramatiques in March 1968. The reaction was instant and electrifying. The play generated so much enthusiasm that, in the euphoric week that followed the reading, five different companies approached the young author for permission to produce *Les Belles-Soeurs*. He decided upon the Rideau Vert, and on 28 August the play was officially premiered.

In the critical battle that ensued, there remained only one point on which all could agree: with *Les Belles-Soeurs,* theatre history had indeed been made. Public and critics alike were forced to ask themselves some far-reaching questions about the relation between art and life in Quebec, in particular the question of what the dramatist ought to examine in society and what language he should use to conduct this examination. Martial Dassylva's review in *La Presse* summed up what was no doubt a majority opinion. He questioned the wisdom of Rideau Vert in having undertaken the production and suggested that it might be a disservice to encourage an admittedly talented young writer to travel along paths of such "crudeness and vulgarity": "c'est la première fois de ma vie que j'entends en une seule soirée autant de sacres, de jurons, de mots orduriers de toilette . . . "[1] ("it is the first time in my life that I hear in a single evening so many curses, swear words, four-letter words and bathroom expressions . . . "). Georges D'Auteuil objected not only to the "detestable language" but also to the "lack of structure" in the new play;[2] and Naim Kattan pointed out the grotesque quality of the characterization, which, in his view, implied a "lack of truth."[3]

So strong was the negative reaction to *Les Belles-Soeurs* that the Quebec Ministry of Cultural Affairs refused to grant the $20 000 subsidy necessary to take the play to Paris, where it had been invited by Jean-Louis Barrault to be performed under the auspices of the Festival des Nations. The government, apparently, did not consider the play "exportable." Tremblay took his modest revenge in the form of an incisive parody of old-fashioned aesthetics, "a beautiful play in one act, written in good French," which appeared in *Le Devoir* and was dedicated to the minister of cultural affairs, Thérèse Casgrain. A year later, in 1973, *Les Belles-Soeurs* received a federal subsidy to travel to Paris, where it played at the Espace Pierre Cardin to enthusiastic audiences, thus proving that it was indeed "exportable."

The French reaction to *Les Belles-Soeurs* is very instructive, for it rides easily over those areas that proved impassable to so many critics in Quebec. According to Jaques Cellard in *Le Monde,* language poses no problem at all: *"Les Belles-Soeurs* sont en joual comme *Andromaque* est en alexandrins, parce qu'il faut une langue à une oeuvre, et une langue forte à une oeuvre forte" (*"Les Belles-Soeurs* is in *joual* as *Andromaque* is in alexandrines, because a work needs a language, and a strong work demands a strong language"). The rest of Cellard's glowing review emphasizes the extraordinary qualities of both text and performance:

Le bon vent du Québec nous apporte avec *Les Belles-Soeurs* un grand moment de théâtre. Puissance du texte, vigueur de la mise en scène, . . . une prodigieuse performance collective d'actrices, un défi scénique magistralement relevé . . . une tragi-comédie classique dans son principe, révolutionnaire dans sa volonté et son expression . . . le texte . . . mérite autant d'être lu que d'être vu.[4] (The good wind which blows from Quebec has brought us with *Les Belles-Soeurs* a great moment of theatre. A powerful text, vigorous production, . . . a tremendous collective performance by the actresses, a challenge to the producer which has been met masterfully . . . a tragicomedy classical in its basis, revolutionary in intention and expression . . . the text . . . deserves to be read as well as seen on stage.)

The genesis of the play, as told by the author, is interesting, for the original idea came almost accidentally. Riding on a bus one day, Tremblay noticed with amusement an advertisement by a chocolate manufacturer announcing a cow-counting contest. The idea struck him as funny and slightly absurd; he could visualize a whole family assembled around the kitchen table, diligently trying to discover the correct number of cows in the picture before them. Carrying the idea further to what seemed to him the utmost in absurdity, he invented the "story" of a poor housewife who wins a million gold bond stamps in a contest. He was much surprised when, having finished the first act, he opened a newspaper and found that his invention had become reality: there was indeed a contest offering a million stamps as first prize! "J'étais abasourdi! Mon concours que je considérais comme le summum de l'absurde devenait réalité!"[5] ("I was flabbergasted! My contest, which I considered the ultimate in absurdity, had become reality!"). The episode bears out Oscar Wilde's dictum that life imitates art.

The play, then, is about Germaine Lauzon, an ordinary working-class housewife in East Montreal (the rue Fabre milieu, of course) who, having won one million gold bond stamps in a contest, invites her sisters, sister-in-law and neighbours for an evening of stamp sticking to fill up her booklets. Tremblay simply removes one wall of Germaine's kitchen and allows the audience to look in on the fifteen women as the party proceeds. The essence of the play lies not in action, but in dialogue. Through the conversations of the characters we are given a thorough, and often frightening, insight into the emptiness and misery of their lives—lives of quiet or less than quiet desperation.

The speeches are organized around a simple plot. The women arrive at Germaine's place, singly and in pairs, and settle down to the stamp-sticking job which is the order of the party. As the evening progresses, they become increasingly irritated by Germaine, who insists on flaunting before them the catalogue full of wonderful things she expects to get for her million stamps. Unable to repress their envy and anger, first one, then all of the women begin to secretly stack away the booklets filled with stamps. Suspense builds towards the end of act 2 when Germaine goes to look in the box meant for the full booklets and finds it nearly empty. In spite of various attempts by the other women to distract her, she quickly realizes what has happened. Confronted with the fact of their theft, the *belles-soeurs* react with total defiance. They now turn not only against Germaine, but against each other as well, and Germaine's kitchen becomes a battleground as the women scramble for all the stamps they can get in a violent free-for-all, which provides a release for all their pent-up envy, hatred and frustration. Finally, everyone goes away, leaving Germaine alone and in tears as she pathetically collects the remaining stray stamps from the floor. The play then moves to an absurdist finale full of irony. The *belles-soeurs* are heard singing "O Canada" outside Germaine's window. Slowly, Germaine gets up from the floor and comes to attention. Slowly her composure returns as she, too, joins in the chorus. And then, oh miracle! to the strains of "O Canada," more gold bond stamps begin to rain down upon her from the ceiling. End of play.[6]

Within this basic framework, several minor plots and one major one also develop. The static quality is relieved by a number of more or less "dramatic" interruptions, such as the comings and goings of Germaine's daughter Linda, who at one point walks out on her mother in defiance, but eventually returns bringing two friends with her. Other "action" is provided by the repeated mishaps involving the unfortunate Olivine Dubuc, a senile ninety-three-year-old who has a way of overturning her wheelchair, spilling the water from her dish and otherwise creating considerable disturbance. The major subplot, however, is a psychological one and centres on Pierrette Guérin, Germaine's youngest sister, and a woman named Angéline Sauvé. Pierrette is the black sheep of the family, an outcast from the rue Fabre crowd because she has chosen to earn her living working in that den of all iniquities, a "club."

At the end of act 1, Pierrette creates a coup de théâtre by suddenly appearing on the scene; her sisters react just as if the devil himself had entered their kitchen. The real climax, however, occurs when she familiarly greets Angéline: it turns out that the two are friends. Angéline, who is, to the best of everybody's knowledge, a most respectable spinster, has been secretly frequenting the club where Pierrette works. In act 2, the centre of attention shifts to a confrontation between Angéline and her shocked best friend of thirty-five years, Rhéauna. We cannot help but be deeply moved as we follow the agonies of Angéline, torn between her genuine affection for Pierrette, her need for the release provided by her weekly visits to the club, and her allegiance to Rhéauna and respectability. Not unexpectedly, the voice of reason eventually wins out and Angéline capitulates before Rhéauna's uncompromising ultimatum.

Pierrette herself provides a slight measure of intense psychological action. Rejected by her "Johnny," out of work and penniless at thirty, she has come "home" in the irrational hope that she will find some sort of help and support from her sisters. She alone aligns herself with Germaine when sisters, sister-in-law and neighbours all turn against her. But Germaine fails to respond and orders Pierrette out of her apartment, having failed (or refused) to realize her sister's desperate need.

A final subplot concerns the problems of one of Linda's friends, Lise, who, between trips to the refrigerator for more cokes, confides that she is pregnant, alone and in despair. Pierrette, who has overheard them, provides Lise with the address of a reliable abortionist, and Lise decides to take the frightening step, much against Linda's protestations.

Les Belles-Soeurs resists simple classification. Like the plays of the Theatre of the Absurd, it relies for its effect more on situation and stage imagery than on story line; but unlike absurdist theatre, which has done away with character as well as plot, it does present the audience with a gallery of realistic personalities. Each of the female characters featured in *Les Belles-Soeurs* is carefully drawn and interesting; there is no one central character. One might describe the play as a contemporary domestic tragedy with a collective, rather than an individual, antihero.

Through the author's unusual ability to create lifelike, fully convincing characters, the audience is irresistibly drawn into the everyday lives of these women with all their petty concerns, cheap pleasures, secret dreams and obvious frustrations. The title of the play indicates the closed nature of the world in which they move; "belles-soeurs" ("sisters-in-law") implies that all of them—the four sisters, the one sister-in-law and the remaining friends and neighbours—share a life so similar that they might as well be members of the same family. The author is presenting us here with the picture of an entire generation of women who have been severely traumatized, both individually and collectively. The bleak group portrait does, of course, correspond to a certain historical reality, and much sociological research has gone into attempts to pinpoint the causes of what amounts to a cultural disease. However, Germaine Lauzon and her friends exist on a level of awareness that makes it impossible for them to define even the symptoms of their general malaise. They only know that for them life, such as it is, is not worth living: a "maudite vie plate." The expression sums up, in one almost untranslatable phrase, all their anger, frustration and impotence.[7]

Maudite vie plate, then, is the central theme or leitmotif around which the entire play is organized; it equally permeates Tremblay's later plays of the rue Fabre—or family life—cycle. Nevertheless, in *Les Belles-Soeurs* the author has given greater prominence to the *maudite vie plate* theme than in any of the other plays, not only by repeating the phrase throughout the dialogue so that it becomes an ever-present undercurrent, but also by formally isolating it through a stylized choral recitation in each act: the *maudite vie plate* chorus of act 1 (theme song of the play) and the ode to bingo in act 2. The theme itself is in no way original, however; it is one of the most central concerns of

québécois dramaturgy. The author's uniqueness lies in his hand-
ling of the theme.

Tremblay's chief merit as an artist lies in his ability to
achieve originality through the synthesis of a wide variety of
elements, both new and traditional. This immediately raises
the question of "influences." Tremblay willingly points out his
favourite writers: "Il y a Shakespeare évidemment à cause de
mon grand amour pour les monologues qui n'en finissent plus.
Il y a eu les Grecs à cause des choeurs, pis il y a eu
Beckett . . . "[8] ("Obviously, there is Shakespeare because of my
great love for unending monologues. There were the Greeks,
because of the choruses, then there was Beckett . . ."). However, it must be understood that the influence of these writers
and any others within the tradition of western theatre functions
strictly on an unconscious level. Dramatic techniques and
devices borrowed from the ancient Greeks or from Beckett have
become integral elements in the work of Tremblay only because they had first become an integral part of the author's
conscious — and eventually unconscious — mind. Thus he is
able to combine the most disparate structural components in a
synthesis that appears perfectly unified and of one piece.

His style brings together the two polar opposites of the theatrical tradition: naturalism, the attempt to create the illusion
of a slice of "real life" on stage, and theatricalism, the use of
devices frankly intended to remind the spectators that they are
watching a "performance." Naturalism is achieved through the
characters, situations, settings and the levels of language.
Theatricalism encompasses many and varied techniques: the
stylization of the Greek chorus; the alienation effects of Brechtian epic theatre; the whole range of techniques of the modern
antirealistic theatre, from Pirandello to Beckett. In *Les Belles-
Soeurs*, we can see how all of these are combined into an
effective whole: the naturalistic quality of the basic plot, characters and language used; the transformation of an essentially
naturalistic group — five ordinary housewives — into a stylized
chorus; the alienation effect achieved by the spotlighted
monologues; the absurdist effect of the rain of stamps at the
finale of the play.

As for dramatic structure, a basic distinction must be
made right away. Analyzing the plays of Michel Tremblay,

one comes to the conclusion that they are developed along two separate structural principles — they are based, in fact, on what I would like to call an "inner" as well as an "outer" structure. The inner structure of the plays is determined by the author's method of composition, which, in keeping with his highly auditory type of imagination, is more akin to musical than literary or dramatic creation. As structural elements within each play, the characters function and interact as would voices or instruments in a musical composition. Tremblay's particular method of composition, then, determines the character of the dialogue in his plays as well as their inner structure, which is consciously elaborated by the artist.

The "outer" structure of the plays follows basic conventional patterns. One might be tempted to assume that dramatic works structured along the principles of musical composition would acquire a rather amorphous quality and be lacking in rational development. However, this is not so in the case of Tremblay, whose plays invariably follow the classical model of beginning, middle and end. This rational aspect is further enhanced by their basic classical conception: all the plays either run through without a break, like the Greek tragedies, or, if they are divided into two acts, act 2 usually takes up exactly where act 1 left off (as in *Les Belles-Soeurs*); thus the plays maintain an essential unity. *Les Belles-Soeurs*, like several of Tremblay's plays, not only makes use of the classical unities of time and place but even achieves "perfect" unity, in that length of performance is exactly equal to the length of dramatic action. The classical conception is confirmed by strict adherence to unity of place: all of the action is set in the kitchen of Germaine Lauzon's apartment.

Since the play combines a large number of both realistic and theatrical elements, one can see in its structure at least three levels of plot. On the simplest level, *Les Belles-Soeurs* is a story about a woman who has won a million stamps, invites her sisters and friends to help her paste them into booklets, and eventually discovers that the women have stolen almost all the booklets instead of depositing them into the box provided. On this level, all of the elements are strictly realistic: the setting, a kitchen in a typical working-class tenement building in East Montreal; the language, a heightened and therefore more picturesque and convincing stage version of the *joual* spoken by the city proletariat; the characters themselves, like the language, heightened into sometimes grotesque caricatures, but fully retaining verisimilitude. The plot on this first level is simple and logical:

Exposition: the scene between Germaine and her daughter Linda. Germaine informs Linda that the stamps have arrived and that there will be a "stamp-sticking" party tonight.

Main part of the play: arrival of the guests, settling down to the job. Inciting moment: Mme Brouillette's decision to steal. Rising action: all the women follow suit. Climax: Germaine discovers what has been going on. Dénouement: Germaine is left alone without her stamps.

Surprise finale (a special feature of many of Tremblay's plays): the rain of stamps.

Obviously, this skeleton structure leaves out many elements essential to the play. Viewed on a second level, the play uses the basic plot of Germaine's stamp tragedy as a framework to present a panoramic view of the life of working-class women, through a number of slice-of-life episodes and psychological minidramas worked into the structure of the play, with the story of Angéline Sauvé and Pierrette as the main focus. On this level, the division into acts becomes significant:

ACT I

Exposition: Germaine and Linda

Main part of the play: (1) Arrival of Mme Brouillette (jealousy); arrival of Germaine's sisters Rose and Gabrielle, and the ladies Yvette Longpré and Lisette de Courval. Commentary on the miseries of everyday life. Arrival of the Dubucs, mother-in-law and Thérèse. Episodes involving the senile old woman; stories of the spinster, Des-Neiges Verrette. Arrival of Linda and her friends. Contrast between older and younger generation. (2) Arrival of the ladies Angéline Sauvé and Rhéauna Bibeau from the funeral parlour. (3) Surprise appearance of Pierrette Guérin, the "fallen" sister who reveals she knows Angéline from the club. The act ends on a note of shock and general consternation.

Act 2

The Angéline drama. The drama of Lise Paquette. The Pierrette drama. Dénouement, surprise finale.

Finally, *Les Belles-Soeurs* operates on a third level of meaning as a result of many theatrical devices which lift it above the naturalistic level. These devices serve to bring out a second and more important reality in the lives of the characters beyond the façades created through the realistic dialogue. The audience is introduced to the theatrical from the very start through the use of special lighting effects. Although all characters remain on stage virtually throughout the play, individual scenes are created by spotlighting pairs or groups of characters, while the rest of the stage disappears in darkness. Similarly, the ultra-realistic dialogue acquires a nonrealistic dimension when several characters are grouped together as a chorus many times throughout the play, an effect which underlines their unanimity on the subject under discussion. The most important theatrical devices incorporated into the realistic framework, however, are (1) the two choral recitals in the style of the Brechtian ballad—one per act—which interrupt the "plot" with a definite alienation effect (the *maudite vie plate* chorus and the ode to bingo); (2) a series of highly stylized monologue sequences in which individual characters, singled out by spotlights and alienated by a change in acting style, address the audience, revealing their more intimate and normally hidden selves; and (3) the finale. As a synthesis of realistic and theatrical elements, the structure of the play could be represented as follows:

Realistic level	*Theatrical level*
Act I	
Exposition	
Arrival of first five women	Quintet: "Une Maudite Vie plate" (22ff.)
Conversations, quarrels, Mme Dubuc	Rose Ouimet: the daughter-in-law (37ff.)

Conversations (contests)	Yvette Longpré: the wedding cake (45ff.)
Conversations (fur coats, etc.)	Des-Neiges Verrette: the brush salesman (52ff.)
Quarrels	Lisette de Courval: "cheap" people (59)
Rhéauna, Angéline arrive	The three sisters: *maudit* Johnny (68ff.)
Pierrette appears	

ACT 2

Horror at the idea of the club	Angéline: confession (81ff.)
	Yvette Longpré: party, catalogue of guests (82ff.)
Conversations (parish activities)	Quintet: "L'Ode au bingo" (86ff.)
Lise drama, Pierrette drama	Pierrette, Lise: I don't know what's going to become of me (94ff.)
Conversations (morality)	Rose: *maudit cul*/goddamn sex (101ff.)
Germaine discovers the theft; battle.	

"O Canada"
Rain of stamps

As this model shows, the stylized monologue sequences are a counterpoint to the realistic episodes, and serve to reveal deeper levels of a certain problem: for example, the realistic episode of the women's utter horror at the idea of a respectable lady like Angéline frequenting a "club" is counterpointed by Angéline's confession about the frustration of her joyless life and the relief afforded by her visits to the club; similarly, Rose Ouimet's intransigent attitudes towards morality and her intolerance about unwed mothers find an explanation in the parallel *maudit cul* speech, which reveals her own private sexual trauma. The two major choral recitations serve as leitmotifs for the play as a whole.

Just as the overture of a musical work introduces the listener to the main themes to follow, the *maudite vie plate* chorus of *Les Belles-Soeurs* suggests the play's underlying theme at the very beginning. Before the action starts (Germaine is still in her bedroom struggling with her corset), the first five women to arrive line up facing the audience and announce "Quintette: Une maudite vie plate!" The recitative then alternates between a solo voice and a chorus of four. The catalogue of the women's despised *vie plate* is predictably mundane: the women call out the days of the week one by one and enumerate the chores for that particular day, emphasizing the endless repetition and frustration. Monday the wash, Tuesday the ironing. Wednesday, shopping day; Thursday and Friday, more of the same. Saturday, the children are home from school to make matters worse; Sunday means eating out at the mother-in-law's. The routine of the week never changes any more than does the routine of individual days, which are inescapably tied to an unending round of breakfast, lunch and dinner. Television provides the only semblance of relief at the end of the daily routine: "Pis le soir, on regarde la télévision!" Obviously, the same basic daily round could as easily have been given a positive, even an idyllic interpretation — after all, the women are describing nothing less than the very essence of the traditional ideal of the family, which supposes a woman's devotion to her sacred duties as wife and mother. What a romantic writer would have depicted as a small paradise, Tremblay paints as hell itself.

The real problem, of course, lies less in the activities themselves than in the women's attitudes towards these activities. The single most striking element in their litany of daily life is the total absence of any positive emotion, let alone love. Throughout the entire "poem," we feel that the women act in a kind of blind rage at being trapped like the cogs of a machine that keeps them going whether they like it or not. Each activity is seen as a chore to be performed simply because "it is there" and must be done, never because it will contribute to the well-being of another person, husband or child. All intimations of family life are negative: the woman is tired and cranky; children come home bringing with them dirt, noise and disorder; husbands, if they are home at all, fill one function only, partners to quarrel with. The sense of hatred towards the family that emanates from the choral recitation is positively frightening: "J'm'esquinte, j'me désâme, j'me tue pour ma gang de nonos!" (23-24) ("I cut myself to pieces, I sacrifice myself, I kill myself for my gang of idiots!"). Modern literature generally does not take kindly to the institution of the family, but nowhere perhaps has it been treated with such devastating cruelty as in the *maudite vie plate* chorus. It is an ode not only to the difficulties of daily living but also to the emotional impotence engendered by family living. Here we come back to the concept of the need for transcendence which, we have seen earlier, forms an integral part of Tremblay's dramatic universe. The *belles-soeurs* are clearly unable to formulate this need though they feel the inadequacies of their life and respond with anger, hatred and rebellion.

The effectiveness of the *maudite vie plate* ode is enhanced by a number of clever technical devices. Tremblay launches his chorus on a note of linguistic satire that underlines the discrepancy between idealized and actual "reality." Lisette de Courval's initial solo is written in a flowery, mock-classical French, and is quickly interrupted by the *joual* quartet of the other women:

LISETTE DE COURVAL: Dès que le soleil a commencé à caresser de ses rayons les petites fleurs dans les champs et que les petits oiseaux ont ouvert leurs petits becs pour lancer vers le ciel leurs petits cris...

LES QUATRE AUTRES: J'me lève, pis j'prépare le déjeuner! Des toasts, du café, du bacon, des oeufs. J'ai d'la misère qu'l'yable à réveiller mon monde.

(23)

(LISETTE DE COURVAL: As soon as the sun has begun to caress with its rays the little flowers in the fields and the little birds have opened their little beaks to send heavenward their little peeps...

THE FOUR OTHERS: I get outa bed and get breakfast. Toast, coffee, bacon and eggs. I have hell's own time to get everybody up.)

With the introduction of reality also comes the emphasis on repetition, the catalogue of each day's hateful drudgery terminating in the "pis le soir on regarde la télévision" refrain. Throughout the recitation, Tremblay, as usual, has captured the rhythms of spoken language magnificently; this linguistic naturalism is punctuated at regular intervals by the stylized announcement of each day of the week, which is shouted out at the audience in a manner evoking a barker at a fair. In contrast to the satirical tone of the introduction, the chorus ends with a highly emotional outburst, which, like the private monologues of the play, confronts the audience with the true feelings of the characters: "Chus tannée de mener une maudite vie plate! Une maudite vie plate! Une maudite vie plate!" ("I've had it with this god-damn rotten life!").

The same basic theme underlies the major ode of act 2, the ode to bingo. As in the earlier ode, the author uses the formal device of a choral recitation to set out in relief one particularly important idea; here, it is the pathetically petty and vulgar activity that gives the *belles-soeurs* their greatest pleasure in life — the weekly parish bingo. A better illustration of the *maudite vie plate* could hardly have been found: life must be arid indeed when a bingo game comes to represent the peak of excitement!

There is enormous pathos in the electrifying effect of the word "bingo" on the assembled women; even old Mme Dubuc awakens from her somnolent state and tries to get into the act. Whereas the mention of children and husbands did not arouse a spark of emotion in the earlier chorus, we now find the women in a veritable frenzy of excitement: "Moé, j'aime ça le bingo! Moé, j'adore le bingo! Moé, y'a rien au monde que j'aime plus que le bingo!" (86) ("Me, I just love bingo! Me, I adore bingo! Me, there's nothing in the world I like better than bingo!"). The same refrain is repeated several times, with increasing intensity, throughout the ode. This near-orgasmic frenzy rises to a nine-voice crescendo as the poem climaxes in an outburst over the ultimate rewards of playing bingo — the prizes they might win: "Vive les chiens de plâtre! Vive les lampes torchères! Vive le bingo!" ("Hurrah for plaster dogs! Hurrah for floor lamps! Hurrah for bingo!").

The combination of realistic/naturalistic with theatrical/ stylized elements provides *Les Belles-Soeurs* with a highly complex structure on three levels. In order to really understand the inner workings of the play, however, we have to go another step and look at the "inner" structure, the elements of musical composition on which it is based. In his review of *Les Belles-Soeurs* for *Le Monde*, Jaques Cellard called the play an "oratorio" — and the term is well chosen. The work is based on fifteen voices which are treated much like the voices in a musical composition. There are ensemble effects, as well as a number of important solo parts (the monologues discussed earlier). Voices are used singly or combined in groups of two or more for special effects. "Une Maudite Vie plate" is a quintet; "L'Ode au bingo," also a quintet, is enhanced by the single voices of four more women, who shout out the numbers of the bingo game as the quintet pursues its recital. Variations on a theme eventually lead to a summation taken up by several voices in unison. Thus, the discussion about the ingratitude of children climaxes in a chorus of "Que c'est donc ingrat, les enfants, que c'est donc ingrat!" (36) ("How ungrateful kids are, how ungrateful!"). A perfect example of the use of voices to develop themes occurs in act 2, where the women discuss the problem of the "club." This passage also provides an interesting example of Tremblay's use of counterpoint:

RHEAUNA BIBEAU (*solô* 1): Angéline! le club, mais c'est l'enfer!

PIERRETTE GUERIN (*solô* 2): Si l'enfer ressemble au club ousque j'travaille, ça m'fait rien pantoute d'aller passer mon éternité là, moé!

GERMAINE, ROSE, GABRIELLE (*trio* 1): Farme-toé, Pierrette, c'est le diable qui parle par ta bouche!

LINDA, GINETTE, LISE (*trio* 2): Le diable? voyons donc!... C'est ben l'fun, les clubs!

(78)

(RHEAUNA BIBEAU [*solo* 1]:Angéline! But the club means hell!

PIERRETTE GUERIN [*solo* 2]: If hell looks like the club where I work, I wouldn't mind spending my eternity there, not a bit!

GERMAINE, ROSE, GABRIELLE [*trio* 1]: Shut up, Pierrette, it's the devil speaking through your mouth!

LINDA, GINETTE, LISE [*trio 2*]: The devil? Come on, now!...
Clubs are great fun!)

Another musical device is the use of a refrain that runs
through portions of the text as a minor leitmotif. Thus,
Gabrielle's "J'ai-tu l'air de quequ'un qui a déjà gagné
quequ'chose!" (41) ("Do I look like someone who's ever won
anything!") is taken up subsequently by the voices of Rose,
Thérèse and others.

The ultimate success of the play from a technical point of
view, and the overall effect of unity and harmony which it
achieves, is no doubt due to this effective orchestration of the
fifteen voices into a harmonious composition which provides
the inner structure, in fact, the very essence (one is tempted to
say, the soul) of the work. It is through the successful manipulation of the voices that the characters of *Les Belles-Soeurs* come
alive. By contrast, the formal, external structural pattern
appears almost insignificant, despite its complexity.

Through the characters and situations which carry the
central theme, the social message of *Les Belles-Soeurs* comes
through with powerful force. Even on this most basic level of
interpretation, the author's use of the theatre as a sociological
instrument is apparent at once. By exposing a particular
stratum of society, the world of the East Montreal housewife,
and displaying it devoid of all protective covering, Tremblay
achieves an immediate double effect of shock and recognition.
He forces his audience to submit to a kind of identification
therapy which is bound to result in a serious *prise de conscience,* a
sort of collective stocktaking of social and moral values. Beyond
the desire to *épater les bourgeois*, always present in avant-garde
works, Michel Tremblay's first great play gives evidence of a
very firm intention to expose an untenable situation.

On the level of moral, or socio-political, allegory, one
might point to the significance of the fact that the author presents us with an all-female society. The world of women, a
powerless, exploited and almost marginal group in traditional
society, effectively parallels the position of Quebec as a whole
versus the rest of the North American continent. However, one
should not make too much of such an allegory, for there are

other and more practical reasons for the preponderance of females in the Tremblay universe. First of all, there is the author's personal background. He himself grew up in just such a setting, surrounded by women,[9] which has no doubt made him particularly sensitive to the special nuances of the female world, and he is quick to transpose his particular and often unusual insights onto the dramatic plane. There is also the possible influence of the fact that, historically, Quebec has been a largely matriarchal society. As Carl Jung has suggested, "The mother complex is very frequent in America. It is heavily accentuated because of the strong predominance of maternal influence as well as because of the position usually given to women."[10]

Beyond its powerful cultural appeal, the play also works at a basic, universal level by illustrating the vigorous, if ineffectual, protests of human beings caught in the grip of a deadly routine from which they do not know how to escape. There is an existentialist anguish and despair in the *belles-soeurs*, but although they are conscious of the absurdity of life, they cannot reach the existentialist state of grace, the discovery of their own freedom.

In spite of its merits, the play almost failed to see the light of public performance and suffered a prolonged series of trials and tribulations in the course of its production history, largely on account of Tremblay's pioneering use of *joual* as a dramatic idiom.

Although, as we have seen, his use of Montreal slang on stage was immediately interpreted as a political act, there was nothing political in Tremblay's original decision to write in *joual*. He had started out using the classical French he had learned in school, assuming, as did his contemporaries, that it was normal for a writer in Quebec to live and think in one language and to compose in another. This kind of aesthetic schizophrenia was bound to produce a certain malaise in the sensitive young author; but the malaise remained largely unconscious until, almost by accident, he stumbled upon the solution to the problem. He had always been a great cinema fan, but French-Canadian productions had a way of making him feel uncomfortable. One day in 1964, after watching a double feature of films by Pierre Patry, he and his friend André Brassard suddenly "saw the light": "On a eu le flash en même temps,"[11] as he later put it. The trouble with these films was that the people in them did not speak the language of the people in real life. It was a revelation: "D'un seul coup, je suis passé aux antipodes de ce que j'avais toujour cru"[12] ("Suddenly, I went from what I had always believed to the absolute opposite"). He went home, sat down at his desk and, with surprising speed, wrote *Les Belles-Soeurs*.

Joual had, of course, appeared in French-Canadian literature earlier, with the novelists and poets of the Parti Pris movement of 1963; but until 1968, it was considered unfit for a medium as public and wide open as the theatre. Where *joual* had been used on stage, it was mainly for the purposes of parody or contrast. For example, Eloi de Grandmont used it in his adaptation of Bernard Shaw's *Pygmalion* as an effective way to transpose into French the cockney speech of Eliza Doolittle. In Réjean Ducharme's *Le Cid maghané*, a parody of Corneille's well-known classic, *joual* alternates with the purist French as a means of accentuating the difference between the two styles of language and, by extension, the two cultures. In each of these instances, *joual* serves only a specific and partial function within the dramatic structure; it remained for Tremblay to elevate it to the rank of a full-fledged dramatic idiom.

The linguistic controversy over Tremblay's play raged continuously for many years and to such an extent that it almost completely eliminated critical consideration of other, and perhaps more important, aesthetic issues. His use of *joual* not only set off a series of literary shock waves, but also raised questions concerning the political realities of life in Quebec. Some critics considered the inadequacies of the popular idiom compared to classical French a humiliating reminder of Quebec's sorry political status; therefore, Tremblay's use of it constituted an act of "abdication." Others believed that using *joual* in the theatre represented a conscious acceptance and definition of Quebec's identity as a North American nation; thus, Tremblay's play marked the first step towards decolonization and liberation. Tremblay himself had simply sought the most suitable idom with which to give imaginative expression to certain characters and situations, and had found that idiom in *joual*. He was not unaware of the wider implications of his choice of language, of course; but his motivation was, at first, predominantly artistic and not political. *Les Belles-Soeurs* became a test case of sorts. With the success of the play in Paris, the process of its canonization at home rapidly gathered momentum. Not only that, but the increasing acceptance by the Quebec public of the other Tremblay plays which followed in rapid succession paved the way for the experimental and avantgarde theatre of the seventies. Now, more than ten years later, the debate about the use of *joual* has died down. In fact, the term itself is seldom used any longer. The breakthrough that Tremblay and his immediate successors achieved in making the language of the people acceptable as a dramatic idiom has contributed to a widespread acceptance of the vernacular—now simply called *québécois*. Tremblay himself no longer refers to the language of his plays as *joual*, but as *québécois*.

Because curses occur so frequently in the *joual/québécois* context, and because, as we have seen, they are difficult to render in English, a word of explanation is in order here. The range, complexity and colour of Québécois swearing far exceeds anything the English language can possibly offer. The most important difference, of course, lies in the origin: French-Canadian swear words tend to be taken from the terminology of religion and liturgy, whereas English curses are by and large scatological. Québécois swearing knows three distinct levels: the *juron* is just an ordinary curse, such as "maudit," "bâtard," and "verrat," easily translated as "damned," "bastard" and "pig." The *sacre* is the most common form of swearing, and involves the use of a religious expression, the most common being "câlice," "calvaire," "Christ" (also spelled "crisse"), "ciboire," "hostie," "sacrement" and "tabernacle." Out of this basic repertoire of seven nouns, an astounding variety of *sacres* can be created by variations in spelling, combinations of two or more *sacres* into one breathtaking string, or the transformation of the nouns into verbs which can be recombined with other nouns for more effect. The possibilities are legion and Tremblay is well aware of them all. The third level is that of the *blasphème*, which involves preceding one of the *sacres* with the word "maudit."

Tremblay sustains the *maudite vie plate* motif of *Les Belles-Soeurs* by exploiting linguistic realism to the full. Every one of the *sacres* occurs profusely in the speeches of the fifteen women, who thus emerge in all their pathetic ignorance and vulgarity. In cursing, these females are the equal of any man; they swear their way through all the levels of censored speech, from "maudite vie" and "verrat de bâtard" to every combination of "câlice," "crisse," "hostie" and "calvaire." The vulgar tone inherent in such profuse swearing is accentuated by the proliferation of crude, often scatological language, such as "manger d'la marde" ("eat shit"), "chier sur le monde" ("shitting on people"), "agace-pissette" ("cock-teaser") and the constantly repeated "ta yeule" or "farme ta yeule" ("shut up"). Certain standard phrases, found in the mouth of practically every one of the *belles-soeurs*, are indicative of a common state of mind: "chus tannée" or "que chus donc tannée" ("I'm fed up"); "j'ai mon voyage" ("I've had it"); "bonrien," "bonrienne" ("good-for-nothing"). Redundancies in the expressions used suggest naiveté: "ça n'a pas de saint grand bon sens" ("it doesn't make a whole lot of sense"), or "le bon Dieu du ciel" ("the good Lord in heaven"). At the same time, such redundant expressions lend a picturesque quality to the language of the *belles-soeurs*. Actually, many of the expressions, *joual* or French, that they use quite spontaneously have a highly poetic quality, owing to their picturesque imagery: "je tire le diable par la queue" ("I can hardly make ends meet"); "je n'aime pas les messes basses" ("I don't like whispering"); "il se fend le cul en quatre" ("he's working himself to death"). There is also an element of unconscious humour, as the women misuse words that are beyond the context of their daily lives, such as "étoile" for "étole" ("stole"). Finally, frequent repetitions render the flavour of spontaneous speech, especially that of the poorly educated. All the *belles-soeurs* have a tendency to ride a word to death. Mlle Des-Neiges Verrette, for example, announcing the prizes to be expected at her brush demonstration: "Y donne des belles tasses fancies à celle qui fait la démonstration.... Des vraies belles tasses de fantaisie ... Vous devriez les voir, sont assez belles!" ("He gives out lovely cups and saucers to the one who hosts the demonstration, really lovely fancy ones ... just lovely ... you should just see them, I tell you, lovely!"). Germaine Lauzon, too, has a special habit of repeating things several times, especially when she is excited.

The total impact of Tremblay's particular adaptation of *joual* as a stage idiom, with its combination of vulgarity, linguistic limitation and limitations in thought, is a sense of intellectual and emotional impotence, which underlines the central theme of the play. Each one of the *belles-soeurs* appears condemned without hope of reprieve to a *maudite vie plate* indeed. Marie-Ange Brouillette's statement at the beginning of the play effectively sums up each of the "sisters'" attitude towards life: "Moé, j'mange d'la marde, pis j'vas en manger toute ma vie" ("As for me, I eat shit, and I'll be eating shit for the rest of my life").

CHAPTER FOUR

Debunking a Myth: Tremblay's Unholy Families

With *Les Belles-Soeurs* and its *maudite vie plate* motif, Michel Tremblay laid the thematic foundation on which he would erect his future dramatic structures. The plays that followed developed along two parallel lines: the rue Fabre cycle (the family) and the Main cycle (those who have escaped from the family). Then, in the latest plays, *Sainte Carmen de la Main* and *Damnée Manon, Sacrée Sandra*, the two opposite poles come together in a fusion and expansion of themes which carry these works beyond the earlier plays to a level of philosophical and metaphysical significance. The evolution of Tremblay's dramatic opus proceeds along such clear lines that they form an almost pyramidal pattern:

Towards Mysticism

Damnée Manon, Sacrée Sandra
Sainte Carmen de la Main

Hosanna	*A toi, pour toujours, ta Marie-Lou*
Trois Petits Tours	*Bonjour, là, bonjour*
Demain matin, Montréal m'attend	*En pièces détachées*
La Duchesse de Langeais	*Les Belles-Soeurs*

THE MAIN   THE RUE FABRE

As we have seen already in *Les Belles-Soeurs*, Tremblay's foremost preoccupation is with the family. This seems only logical, since as a playwright he must deal not with philosophical or sociological abstractions, but with concrete human situations — and the family represents a hub, a focal point, where many social ills and their effects on individuals converge and can be easily exposed to view. In his works, the family is seen as both a product and a source of collective as well as personal traumas. If liberation of an entire society depends upon the liberation of the individuals who make up the society, then it can be achieved only by freeing the individual from the bondage of the family. In Tremblay's words, "I most often write about the family because I want to put a bomb in the family cell. I hate what the family did to me and what the institution of the family did to my people"; [1] his statement echoes Gide's much-quoted "familles, je vous hais!" ("families, I hate you!").

Such a negative attitude towards the institution of the family is by no means unique in modern literature; it is a commonplace in the late twentieth century, and can be traced back to Strindberg, Ibsen and Wedekind in the nineteenth. Margaret Atwood has examined the treatment of the family in the literature of English Canada and has concluded that it is most often portrayed as "a trap" from which it is virtually impossible to escape. [2] Her image applies perfectly to the literature of French Canada; in fact, it appears verbatim in *A toi, pour toujours, ta Marie-Lou*, when Carmen refers to the institution of the family as "c'te maudite trappe à rats" ("this goddamn rat trap"). It must also be pointed out that the reaction against an idyllic treatment of the family occurred with greater violence in French than in English Canada, simply because the myth of the "holy family" had been imposed upon that society for a considerably longer period, and with much more force.

It is not difficult to find reasons for the excessive emphasis on the family, especially the large family, throughout the history of French Canada. The reasons are political as well as social, economic and religious, and date back at least to the time of the Conquest. When the French Canadians found themselves defeated at the hands of the British and reduced to the status of a small and politically insignificant cultural minority, their reaction was to adopt an aggressive defensiveness, a stance of *survivance-résistance:* and certainly the "survivance" could be best achieved by outdoing the birth rate of the conqueror. In this way, the "revanche du berceau" ("revenge of the cradle"), as it was later called, came into being as a nationalistic policy of survival. And it worked extremely well: following the Conquest, French Canada showed the highest birth rate ever recorded for a white population (65.3 per 1000). The large family, then, became a symbol of patriotic fervour, embodying the highest moral value. The trend towards large families with its concomitant idealization of motherhood was further fostered by the peculiar socio-economic development of French Canada, which remained largely agricultural long after the rest of the North American continent had changed to a predominantly urban and industrial lifestyle. Even after the industrialization of Quebec and a large-scale population shift to the cities, the working-class districts of these cities tended to retain a village atmosphere: in Maisonneuve, Verdun, Lachine, even East Montreal, the first generation, at least, of new arrivals perpetuated the narrow isolationism of the rural life they were used to. Finally, the Catholic Church played a major part in upholding the holiness of motherhood and the family throughout French-Canadian history, encouraging large families and the "simple life" of agriculture. "Religion, the family, agriculture and private property" were presented to the French-Canadian population as the cornerstones of eternal salvation as well as temporal prosperity, well into the forties.[3] Since the Church also held a monopoly on education and intellectual leadership, it influenced very strongly the developing literature of French Canada. No wonder, then, that this literature should have been predominantly regional — peasant or *terroir* literature idealizing family life and the cultivation of the soil. Such idyllic trends were kept alive in the period between the two world wars by major literary magazines like *Le Canada Français, Le Terroir* and *Le Pays Laurentien*, which often reinforced the written message with pictures illustrating the virtues of a fruitful domestic life spent on the land.

When French Canadians began to develop a national dramaturgy, in the form of radio drama, it naturally took up the idyllic treatment of the family from the preceding literary forms. Marriage in these plays is seen in an almost mystical light, the final *inveni portum,* haven of the weary wanderer through life. Man's quest ends when the union between husband and wife is complete. Woman, in her function as wife and mother, is idealized as the power that lifts man's life out of the ordinary into a realm which marries physical contentment to spiritual transcendence.

With *Fridolinons*, Gélinas's satirical revues of the forties, reality finally broke through the romantic idyll of the family that French-Canadian literature had constructed for so long. In a number of sketches such as *Aurore's Wedding* and *They Lived Happily Ever After*, Gélinas dared expose the realistic side of marriage and parenthood: grumbling, ineffectual fathers; harassed mothers; impotent and/or rejected husbands, and their counterpart, frustrated and/or frigid wives. In the traditionally bold genre of the satirical revue, at least, the central taboo of French-Canadian society had been broken. The debunking of the myth of the holy family could now begin in earnest.

With the general clearing of the air at the end of the Duplessis era and the advent of the Quiet Revolution, a realistic approach to the problems of family life and sexuality at last became possible on the stage. As was to be expected after a long period of repression, the reaction was instantaneous, and vicious. Throughout the sixties, Marcel Dubé held the central spot in the theatrical life of Montreal. His psychological dramas presented a seemingly endless array of monstrous families, of which the most striking examples occur in *Bilan* (1960), *Au Retour des oies blanches* (1966) and *Les Beaux Dimanches* (1968). Each one of these features a family torn by hatred and contempt, corrupt to the core, a living hell for all of its members. Yet, the work of Dubé comes nowhere near the impact achieved by Michel Tremblay when he sets out to dissect the psychology and physiology of the family unit. Dubé's plays retain a kind of surface polish which softens their effect on the audience: because they are set in sophisticated upper bourgeois households and are written in "good" French, they seem more like boulevard plays, without the immediacy achieved by Tremblay.

By setting his family plays in a working-class milieu, and reinforcing the naturalistic effect of the setting with the use of a merciless *joual* throughout, Tremblay forces on his audience a greater sense of "reality" than that produced by any previous French-Canadian dramatist. The problems of family life become more accentuated, of course, if they are seen against a background of sordid living conditions at home and deadly repetitious routine at work, as opposed to a milieu of suburban living and professional occupations. Pierre Vallières understood this very well when he wrote, "la famille bourgeoise est une monstruosité sociale . . . la famille ouvrière est une double ou quadruple monstruosité . . . un enfer, un huis-clos où l'autodestruction des êtres s'accomplit machinalement par un prolongement automatique de l'exploitation de l'ouvrier par son patron"[4] ("the bourgeois family is a social monstrosity . . . the working-class family is a double or quadruple monstrosity . . . a hell, a closed cell where the autodestruction of human beings is carried on mechanically as an automatic extension of the exploitation of the worker by his employer"). Vallières's analysis might have been made particularly of Tremblay's *A toi, pour toujours, ta Marie-Lou*, it fits the play so exactly; with modifications, it applies to the entire family cycle of plays.

Although *En pièces détachées, Bonjour, là, bonjour* and *A toi, pour toujours, ta Marie-Lou* present three separate and clearly differentiated family units, the three plays share the same basic theme as well as a parallel pattern in the characterization of the three generations appearing in this cycle. In each one of the three plays, the family tragedy is played out against the background of nauseous *vie plate* that we met in *Les Belles-Soeurs;* family relations are a nightmare of painful and negative emotions that result from the total absence of love; and the institution of the family itself is viewed by both older and younger members as a virtually escape-proof trap.

The pattern of characterization is strikingly uniform. In each play, the father figure projects a profoundly pathetic sense of impotence. The physical manifestation of his general impotence varies from play to play, but the symbolism remains remarkably effective: Gérard, the father in *En pièces détachées*, is half-paralyzed and limps about the house with the help of a cane; this physical disability has its intellectual counterpart as well, since he is presented as an almost moronic type. Gabriel, in *Bonjour, là, bonjour*, is deaf and thus cut off from any participation in the activities of the family; his social impotence is underlined by the fact that he is old and retired. Léopold, in *A toi, pour toujours, ta Marie-Lou*, suffers from a streak of hereditary insanity which threatens at any moment to lead him to the absolute impotence of the asylum.

We find the logical counterpart of this gallery of impotent males in a corresponding set of females whose most basic emotion is a deep sense of frustration. This is true of every one of the mother figures in the three plays. Gérard's mother-in-law, Robertine, is the central mother figure in *En pièces détachées*. Her life, as shown through the action of the play and especially through her own long monologue, has been nothing but one unending sequence of disappointments and frustration, all within the confines of the house where she was born, has spent a lifetime trying to cope, and expects to die. In *Bonjour, là, bonjour*, we find two sets of mother figures playing opposite the father, Gabriel. There are, first of all, the two maiden aunts, their spinsterhood the very incarnation of a life of frustration on all levels. In the next generation, we are presented with Gabriel's three older daughters, all of whom play mother to their younger brother, Serge, who thus becomes the target of a threefold sexual frustration, which is in no way relieved by the fact that each one of these younger women is, after all, in official possession of a husband. Finally, Marie-Louise stands out as the epitome of the frustrated and embittered wife and mother, certainly Tremblay's finest creation in this particular genre. Her emotional state is beautifully exteriorized by the visual imagery of the stage. The author places her, a wife, mother of three and expectant mother, in a setting that exudes the spirit of old maidenhood which is Marie-Louise's ideal: a rocking chair in front of the television set, knitting on her lap, and a room filled with statues of saints, candles and similar paraphernalia of spinsterly devotion to religion.

Such marriages of impotence with frustration can produce in their offspring only one desire: to escape from the hell of the parents' making. Most of the children, however, run into a blind alley. Robertine's daughter Thérèse takes to drink, which only serves to aggravate the underlying difficulties of her existence. Gabriel's three older daughters collectively seek an outlet in their close to incestuous interest in their "little brother," and individually in the customary escape routes — the pill bottle for Monique, the refrigerator for Denise and an extramarital affair in the case of Lucienne. Manon, in *A toi, pour toujours, ta Marie-Lou*, does not even wish to escape, but rather spends her life in pious imitation of her dead mother, and through conscious effort relives the sordid family life of her past. None of these characters has understood the true nature of the hell from which they try so ineffectually to escape, which is the absence of love. Three of the third-generation characters have gained at least a dim understanding of the truth and realize that the first step to emotional liberation must be liberation on the sexual level. Manon's sister Carmen knows it well: having broken all the taboos that surround the family, she has made a life for herself as a singer of Western songs on the Main. Boldly confronting Manon with her new-gained freedom, she appears independent, happy and sexually liberated. A similar breakthrough occurs in *Bonjour, là, bonjour*, where we find the only case of genuine romantic love between a young man and a young woman in the entire Tremblay opus; but it is romantic love with a twist. Serge, only son of Gabriel, is in love with Nicole, youngest of his four sisters, who fully returns her brother's feeling. Only after Serge comes to the hard-won decision that he and Nicole must accept the fact of their love for each other and live accordingly, regardless of consequences, if they are to achieve sexual/social liberation, does he become capable of the genuine act of love towards his father that the old man has been waiting for all his life. Carmen and Serge, then, must be seen as the two most fully liberated characters in the family cycle of plays, even if their liberation only extends to the freedom afforded by a job in a cheap cabaret in one case and love-within-the-family in the other. There is no need to elaborate further on the author's pessimistic view of life in general and of life in his own *québécois* society in particular. As Jacques Cotnam has pointed out, "Michel Tremblay est en train de créer une dramaturgie *nationale* authentique, qui reflète les frustrations accumulées depuis trois cents ans..."[5] ("Michel Tremblay is in the process of creating a genuine national dramaturgy which reflects the frustrations accumulated over three hundred years...").

Of the three plays centring on the family, *En pièces détachées* is the author's first chronologically; it goes back to an early version written in 1966, produced before *Les Belles-Soeurs*.[6] As the title indicates (literally, "In Separate Pieces"), the play is loosely structured, being made up of four episodes divided by three choral interludes. However, the focus is considerably less diffuse than in *Les Belles-Soeurs,* since the entire play centres around one family only, that of Robertine. The effect of concentration is enhanced by a classical adherence to the unities of time and place. The entire action takes place in the course of one afternoon and evening. The central setting never changes: "la cour," the inner courtyard with its complement of gossips at their windows who constitute the chorus of the play. For the four scenes from Thérèse's life which make up the episodes of the play, we move to the main locations of her customary activities: the restaurant where she works, the bar where she drinks and the living room where she confronts her mother Robertine and the rest of her family.

Of all the possible reactions to the miseries of living in general and family living in particular, Tremblay has chosen total abdication as the leitmotif for this play, an abdication summed up in the recurring *chus pas capable* refrain of the final monologues. "Chus pas capable" ("I can't any longer") expresses the characters' final sense of defeat in face of the disappointments of the past, the futility of the present and the hopelessness of the future. There is a strong feeling of attrition running through this play—the passing of time which brings with it a slow but inescapable erosion, thus burdening each one of the characters, and the audience, with a vague and painful sense of loss. From this point of view, *En pièces détachées* comes close to the emotional impact created, in a much gentler manner, of course, by the plays of Chekhov and Turgenev. The theme is mainly expressed through the dialogue itself, reinforced by the three "external" elements: setting, story line and characters.

By establishing *la cour*, the inner courtyard, as the central setting for the play, Tremblay immediately creates a *maudite vie plate* background for his domestic tragedy. It is an unbearably hot afternoon in East Montreal. Housewives lounge at their windows in quest of a breeze, guzzling cokes, discussing ail- ments and pregnancies, quarrelling with each other and their husbands, whose beer-swilling presence is felt somewhere in the depths of the house. The general atmosphere is as op- pressive as the heat and produces a general reaction of irrit- ability, hostility and boredom. It is quite obvious that for all of these women, life holds no excitement other than that provided by the well-known, unsavoury goings-on in Robertine's living room. And so, the furies of the rue Fabre wait with ill-con- cealed impatience for Thérèse to come home and for their "show" to go on. Not a shred of human compassion is shown to- wards harassed old Robertine, to whom they refer with quite unconscious callousness as "la folle d'en face" ("the crazy woman across the street").

The other settings provide no relief from the atmosphere inside *la cour*. The stage directions for Nick's delicatessen on rue Papineau, where Thérèse works as a waitress, carefully empha- size the more unsavoury aspects of the food business, the better to contain Thérèse in an environment that is permanently bleak. Thus, Tremblay specifically indicates that no "filled" or "appetizing-looking" plates must be shown, only "dirty dishes, piled up on a cart or in the sink." The scene played in the family living room is set in an atmosphere of shabbiness, poverty and neglect; even the television set is "twelve or thir- teen years old." The only setting that clearly belongs to a better world is the bar, cool and glittering with chrome — but here, of course, we have the lost paradise of Thérèse's barmaid dreams, which she is prevented from entering. Atmosphere, then, is used extensively in this play to convey the general theme.

Tremblay's story line, as always, is extremely simple, a slice-of-life rather than a plot. After an introductory chorus that sets the tone and gives us some information about family life at Robertine's, we find Thérèse, in the first episode, on the job at Nick's. It is immediately apparent that she is on a rapid downhill slide. Although she allows herself the luxury of feeling declassed, having moved from a bar on the Main to a cheap restaurant on rue Papineau, she knows very well that even her present job is by no means secure. After work, she goes on one of her customary drinking sprees and ends up at the Coconut Inn, scene of her earlier glories. Beautiful and poised Lucille, who now holds the rank of barmaid, stands for everything Thérèse covets but is unable to attain. We now discover that Thérèse was literally kicked out of the Coconut Inn because of her heavy debts and her continual drinking. Meanwhile at home, the women are gleefully aware that Thérèse is late returning, and so they look forward to a good "show" since she will obviously return drunk and thus provide a bit of excitement for the neighbours. When she does appear, they are not disappointed. In full hearing of the gloating neighbours, Thérèse bullies and insults both her mother and her husband, only to end the scene in a tearful orgy of self-humiliation. Eventually, she retires to bed.

The next chorus makes us aware of the existence of Thérèse's younger brother, Marcel, inmate of an insane asylum. In the final episode later that night, Marcel, having escaped from the asylum, returns home. The madman, ultimate symbol of alienation, stands in stark contrast to the "normal" members of the family: whereas they are impotent, he feels all-powerful; while they are forever exposed to the scrutiny of each other and the neighbours, he can make himself "invisible"; and in opposition to the bleakness of their environment, Marcel demands that everyone be dressed in white, and that the house be emptied and whitewashed. Following an extraordinarily pathetic scene in which both Robertine, the mother, and Thérèse, the sister, display their love for Marcel with almost painful intensity, the young man is sent back to his asylum and "normal" life resumes, as each character in turn delivers his or her *chus pas capable* monologue. Here, too,

Tremblay resorts to the ever-effective device of a stylized finale to end a naturalistic scene.

As the preceding summary illustrates, *En pièces détachées* shows a certain weakness in construction. The four episodes are only loosely connected, and the unexpected appearance of Marcel as a kind of deus ex machina to add another dimension to the play seems particularly arbitrary. The play does come across as a powerful experience nonetheless, mainly owing to Tremblay's masterful creation of a group of strongly drawn characters.

Each member of the family illustrates in his or her own way the slow erosion and resulting sense of loss which were mentioned previously as central themes of the play. Gérard, husband of Thérèse, is probably the most pathetic case in point. A middle-aged wreck of a man who used to be devastatingly handsome, he has become a prime example of the all-round impotence typical of the males of the Tremblay dramaturgy. Confined to the house ever since an accident that severely limited his mobility (he can only get around with the help of a cane, and then with difficulty), his life has progressively deteriorated and narrowed. By his own admission never a very bright person, he has now sunk into a torpor and slumps in front of the television set all day long, beer in hand. As a defence against the hostility of the three women in the household (his wife, daughter and mother-in law), he has given up communication altogether and prefers to quietly accept their taunts and insults rather than get involved in any way. The only time he shows an interest is when a cartoon program starts on television: the appearance of Popeye, his favourite cartoon character, throws him into a veritable frenzy of enthusiasm — a reaction parallel to that of the *belles-soeurs* at bingo. In his final, private monologue at the end of the play, framed by the "chus pus capable de rien faire!" refrain, Gérard passes in review his life and the madhouse created by "his" three women. He comes to the conclusion that, of the entire family, Marcel alone is well off: "Marcel, lui, au moins, y'est fou pour de vrai! Y'ont pas eu besoin de le rendre fou, celui-là. Lui, y'est fou, pis y'est bien" (90) ("Marcel, at least, he's really crazy! They didn't have to drive him mad, that one. He's crazy, and he's doing alright").

In the character of Thérèse, the sense of loss is even more pronounced, since she started out as an unusually beautiful as well as highly intelligent young girl. However, her life took a downward turn from the moment of her marriage to Gérard. Triumphant over all the other girls in her neighbourhood on her wedding day, she soon found out that her prize catch held no attractions beyond a handsome physique, and even that deteriorated rapidly. Thérèse, then, finds herself forced to support a dead weight of a husband who has given up on life. As she takes to drink to drown out her disappointment over her marriage, her professional life also deteriorates rapidly, and this further contributes to the vicious circle of action and reaction in which she is caught. She appears most pathetic in the episode at the Coconut Inn bar, when she pleads with Lucille to give her back her job there. In a somewhat transparent, but still effectual counterpoint technique, Tremblay sets her dialogue with Lucille against the background of a song being performed on stage, which symbolically reiterates her plight. Her inhibitions lifted by alcohol, Thérèse forgets her pride, and her outcry to Lucille becomes a genuine De Profundis, a cry from the depths of a tortured soul: "Lucille... Lucille... Si tu savais! C'est icitte, ma place, Lucille! C'est icitte que chus t'heureuse!" (41) ("Lucille... Lucille... If you only knew! This is where I belong, right here, Lucille! It's here that I'm happy!").

In the scene that follows, the audience reaction changes from compassion to outrage and disgust at the spectacle of the young woman's drunken violence, her outbursts of hatred and spitefulness against her mother, her utter disdain for her husband and her final self-recrimination amidst a flood of tears. When Marcel appears on the scene, however, she reveals a new facet of her personality. As one of the neighbours comments in the preceding chorus, Marcel may well be "the only person she ever really loved." The only genuine emotion Thérèse is capable of, then, would seem to be an impossible and incestuous love for her insane brother — another gripping example of Tremblay's deeply pessimistic view of human relations. Thérèse's final monologue, like that of Gérard, presents the character in a moment of rare insight ("Aïe, chus rendue basse rare" [9] ["I've sunk pretty low all right"]), since she realizes the full extent of her hatred for everyone in her family and her murderous intentions towards Gérard. However, she also knows very well she will do nothing, as usual: "Chus pus capable de rien faire" concludes her monologue as it does all the others.

Although the limited action of the play revolves around Thérèse, it is her mother Robertine whose character serves as the most eloquent illustration of the theme, simply because she is old and has been forced by circumstances to play the frus- trating role of mother twice over — first to her own children, Thérèse and Marcel, and now to her granddaughter Francine, since Gérard and Thérèse show no inclination to assume the role of parents to their own child. Robertine draws pity the moment she appears on stage; she is a dried-up little old woman in a shabby housecoat who walks bent over with ar- thritis. Following the confrontation with the drunk Thérèse, Robertine delivers a long monologue which the author con- siders "the best thing" he ever wrote. Whether one agrees with this evaluation or not, it is, indeed, a powerful piece of writing which evokes in one short page the pathos of a lifetime of coura- geous "coping" against insurmountable odds:

Rien! Rien pantoute! J'ai rien eu! (*silence*) Rien. Chus venue au monde dans c'te maison-là . . . J'ai eu des parents ignorants, un mari écoeurant . . . Pis des enfants qui sont pas normaux. . . . J'me suis débattue, pourtant! J'ai tellement faite c'que je pouvais! Faut croire que j'pouvais pas grand'chose! (71) (Nothing! Nothing at all! I've had nothing! [*silence*] Nothing. I was born in this house right here, I grew up in this same house, I got married in this same house . . . I've had ignorant parents, a disgusting husband . . . And then children who aren't normal . . . And it's not as if I didn't fight hard! I've done every- thing I possibly could! Must be that I couldn't do much!)

At the end of the monologue, Robertine slips into nostal- gic reminiscences of what must have been the best moments of her life. When Marcel was little, she used to sit out on the bal- cony with him, talking to him endlessly; and Marcel, though he could not understand what she was saying, would listen earnestly and beg her to go on. She ends her reminiscing, and her speech, with a quietly resigned "c'est mieux que rien" ("it's still better than nothing"), which certainly brings out the full pathos of the character. In fact, Tremblay's treatment of Robertine comes dangerously close to sentimentality, here and especially in the final scene with Marcel, when the old woman goes along with the insanities of her son, taking part in an imaginary telephone conservation, putting on the white dress he loves and, finally, promising him he may stay home for good even though she has just called for an ambulance to take him back to the asylum. When she asks his forgiveness "for everything" just as he is about to be taken away, the audience's tolerance for sentiment is taxed to the limit indeed. However, her final speech brings us back with a bang to a more realistic attitude, as she denounces (like the *belles-soeurs* and in the same terms) the vicissitudes of motherhood: "Soyez bonne pour vos enfants, tuez-vous pour eux-autres... Pis vous finirez vot'vie tu-seule, abondonnée, dans un coin, comme une quêteuse, dans votre propre maison" (92) ("Be good to your children, kill yourself for them... You'll still end up your life all alone, abandoned in a corner like a beggar woman, in your own house"). In the final analysis, even Robertine contributes to the debunking of the myth of the loving mother-child relationship.

Bonjour, là, bonjour explores the parent-child, or, in this case, father-son relationship in greater depth. Largely autobiographical and dedicated, in fact, "à mon père," this play is Tremblay's monument to his own father as well as his private version of the archetypal father-and-son story. It takes the form of a one-act play constructed on musical principles, with voices taking the musical parts. The entire piece is made up of thirty-one short sections, numbered and variously entitled "solô," "duo," "trio," and so forth up to "octuor," depending on the number of "voices" (characters) involved in each scene. Tremblay's music-inspired method of composition determines the form of most of his plays; we shall come back to it again, especially in the case of *Sainte Carmen de la Main*. As he himself explains, the method comes to him naturally, a product of his great passion for Brahms.[7] Tremblay is a writer who hears, rather than visualizes, the characters he creates; of *Bonjour, là, bonjour*, he has said that it is "une chose exclusivement sonore pour moi"[8] ("for me, something purely auditory"). In fact, the visual element is absent from the composition to the point that no directions for setting are given at all. Tremblay's voices speak in a vacuum which must be filled in by the imagination of the director. Unity of time is again observed, with events taking place in the course of one afternoon and night. *Bonjour, là, bonjour* is even narrower in focus than *En pièces détachées*. The element of the chorus has been removed, so that our attention is confined entirely to the members of the family under scrutiny.

The central theme of the play is the difficulty of communication in the father-son relationship, with the subtheme of socio-sexual liberation. These themes are played out against the usual background of harried family living. In keeping with the theme, the plot is almost exclusively psychological; there is no physical action. The play centres around twenty-five-year-old Serge, who has just returned to his home and family after a three months' stay in Paris, a trip he undertook to give himself a chance to come to terms with his love for his youngest sister Nicole, thirty. Home and family for Serge means his widowed old father, Gabriel; the two elderly maiden aunts, Charlotte and Albertine, who keep house for him; his three married sisters, and Nicole. From the moment he returns, Serge is overwhelmed by demands from every member of his family — from all but Nicole, who loves him. Fighting off the invasion of relatives, Serge focusses his concern on the two central issues of his life: his strong, but never expressed love for his father and his unorthodox love for his sister. In the course of one stormy evening, he comes to terms with both. Having first decided to fully accept and carry through his relationship with Nicole, come what may, he is then able to break through the long-established communications barrier with his father. At long last, he brings himself to shout the words "I love you" into his deaf father's ear. When he invites Gabriel to move in with him and Nicole, the old man is deeply grateful and overjoyed, even though he is entirely aware of the nature of the relationship between his two children.

Tremblay's father-and-son drama takes place in an atmosphere of frustration, inability to communicate and desire for liberation. The theme of frustration becomes apparent in all the characters and their actions. In the case of Gabriel, it is symbolized by his deafness. Charlotte and Albertine are frustration personified: each one speaks of herself in the third person ("ma tante"), and they often speak in unison, underlining their lack of individuality. Their spinsterish lifestyle itself is a monument to frustration. Albertine claims she has not left the house for five years, and Charlotte evokes pity by constantly calling attention to her innumerable diseases as well as her impecunious state. Too poor to move out of their brother's house, the two old women, who hate each other with a will, are nevertheless forced to share the same bed. Television is their only release; menu planning, the central problem in their lives.

Serge's three older sisters further emphasize the theme of frustration. Lucienne, the eldest, cynically referred to as "l'anglaise" by her sisters, has married an English-Canadian doctor, a move that landed her in the middle of the complex problems of the idle rich — sounding, ironically, quite similar to the ills affecting the less affluent *belles-soeurs*. Lucienne's emotional aridity, in fact, is no different from that of a Germaine Lauzon:

Verrat! vient un temps ousque t'as pus rien à faire! Tu restes assis tes grandes journées de temps, pis ta vie se fait tu-seule, sans toé... Ben, ça m'intéresse pas, moé, de r'garder mes enfants grandir! Chus pas mère-poule pour deux cennes, c'est pas de ma faute! Ça m'intéresse pas, les enfants, ça m'a jamais intéressé. (44) (So what the hell, there comes a time when you've got nothing left to do! There you sit, day in, day out, and your life goes on all by itself without you... Heck, I'm not interested in watching my children grow up! I'm not one bit of a mother hen, it's not my fault! I'm not interested in kids, I never have been.)

Not unexpectedly, Lucienne seeks the outlet of an extramarital affair. There is a comical element in her situation, caught as she is between Bob, her husband, Bobby her son, and Robert her lover — a state of affairs somewhat reminiscent of the absurd proliferation of Bobbys in Ionesco's *Bald Soprano*. Denise, whose husband spends all his time bowling, has settled on a well-stocked refrigerator as a substitute for her stunted emotional life, and as a result she has become so fat that her husband is embarrassed to let her sit at the cash register in the store they own. This character also wavers between the comic and the tragic; she tearfully exclaims, "Ah, pis, laissez-moé donc manger, tout le monde, c'est tout ce qui me reste" (65) ("For God's sake, leave me alone, all of you, and let me eat, it's all I've got left"). Monique, third of the sisters, has been left in charge of an indefinite number of children, and her mother-in-law, by her commercial traveller husband, who is never home. Her method of coping is to go through life in a half-daze brought on by a steady diet of tranquillizers.

Each one of this formidable array of frustrated females zeroes in on Serge, who becomes the target of all their poorly concealed sexual drives. As a combination child/lover figure as well as sex symbol, Serge is overwhelmed by their demands on him, which range from insignificant but irritating admonishments to all-encompassing claims on his life. The women assert the authority they had over him when he was a child: they try to force him to eat, to cut his hair; complain about the way he dresses; fuss over his scarf as he goes out. More dangerously, each one attempts to use Serge for her own purposes: Albertine asks him to take her away; Charlotte demands that he return "home" and threatens to leave unless he does; Lucienne tries to blackmail him into letting her set him up in an apartment, to be used also by herself and her lover; Denise begs hims to stay with her and her family; Monique considers inviting herself to live with him and Nicole. Serge not only must fight off these demands from all sides but he also has to cope with the more openly sexual advances made by his older sisters, especially Denise, who insists on re-enacting the tickling and undressing games of his childhood.

While the theme of frustration is hammered home to the audience in the rather heavy-handed manner described above, the difficulty in communicating is conveyed more subtly. The inability of the characters to "get through" to each other is particularly evident in the form of the dialogues, which could be defined as "centrifugal" in the manner of Chekhov: speech succeeds speech, but no contact is established, because each character pursues his or her private train of thought. The absence of communication becomes especially apparent in those scenes where first Gabriel, then Serge do manage to break through the barrier of inhibitions and tell one another what they have always wanted to say; these speeches (sections 20 and 27) are punctuated by the inane remarks of the two aunts, who blithely continue their chatter, totally oblivious to the importance of what is being said. The lack of communication is further emphasized by the recurrent pattern of one-way conversations: everyone talks, no one listens. There is a slightly comical example of this pattern in the first section, where Serge, having just returned from Paris, is asked to give an account of his travels and then does not get a chance to speak even once. When he finally manages to make himself heard, in section 2, he finds he has nothing to say beyond the most ordinary clichés: "Ah oui, c'est ben beau, Paris! C'est une ville... extraordinaire! C'est grand! Euh... partout ousque tu vas, c'est beau" (31) ("Oh yes, Paris is really beautiful! As a city it's... sensational! It's big! Oh, yeah... wherever you go, it's beautiful"). The lack of communication is also symbolized by Gabriel's deafness. Of all the characters in the play, Serge and Nicole are the only ones who truly communicate with one another, and they can do so even without words. Their secret, of course, is the liberation they achieve through love.

Despite the symphony of failed interpersonal relations evident in *Bonjour, là, bonjour*, Tremblay shows a somewhat more positive attitude towards the possibility of a liberating breakthrough in this play than in any of the others. Serge achieves a genuine liberation both in his relationship with Nicole and in his relationship with his father.

The speeches of Serge and Nicole leave no doubt about the romantic nature of their relationship. The love story is told three times in the course of the play, first by the older sisters, who provide the background, then by Nicole, and finally by Serge. From the older women, we learn how Serge and Nicole, ever since they were small children, have been clinging to each other with a love which the rest of the family first considered "cute" and eventually accepted as somewhat disturbing but unavoidably part of the family configuration. Nicole describes her first fully consummated sexual encounter with her brother, an experience that makes her Tremblay's only romantic heroine:

"Quand c'est arrivé... C'était tellement effrayant, pis tellement beau en même temps... que j'arais voulu qu'on meure tou'es deux, tou-suite après..." (89) ("When it happened... It was so frightening, and so beautiful at the same time... I would have liked for us to die together, afterwards, right away..."). Serge provides a more thoughtful analysis of the situation. Aware of the dangers inherent in so unorthodox a love affair, he has tried hard to free himself, but to no avail. He finally comes to the conclusion that he has no choice: "Pour moé, tout est clair, tout est simple.... C'est de l'amour, pis c'est beau! C'est beau!... On va s'aider à vivre, tou'es deux, pis on va vieillir ensemble" (90) ("For me, it's all clear, it's all simple. ... It's love, and it's great! It's great!... We're going to help each other live, the two of us, and we'll grow old together"). One can hardly imagine a more convincing statement of romantic love.

A similar process of liberation from inhibiting taboos followed by a release of the emotion of love takes place in the relationship between Serge and his father. Gabriel represents a rarity within the Tremblay dramaturgy: an idealized character. In fact, he can be seen as a latter-day version of the archetypal Tiresias, the blind seer. Gabriel cannot hear, but, like Tiresias, he knows all, understands all. He is also shown as an intelligent, well-read man, and a person of great moral courage, who accepts his handicap with quiet resignation. Both father and son suffer equally from their inability to communicate to each other the love they feel. The gradual process of breaking through this barrier of communication is very effectively demonstrated as first one, then the other manages to express his real feelings in the form of a monologue, before the two come together in the dialogue of the last scene. Both monologues are deeply moving; the father expresses his gratitude to the son for providing him with a hearing aid, which has enabled him to experience the joy of music for the first time in forty years, and the son summons all his courage to shout out to his father the message he has wanted to convey all along, "Papa, je t'aime." These scenes, and the final one in which Serge invites his father to come and stay with him and Nicole, are saved from excessive sentimentality by the intrusion of other voices. Both monologues run parallel with Charlotte's and Albertine's chatter. The final dialogue is orchestrated as an "octuor"; the voices of Serge and Gabriel must compete with a cacophony of crisscrossing conversations by all the other members of the family.

Bonjour, là, bonjour can be interpreted on at least three levels. Literally, it is a naturalistic and largely autobiographical family portrait. On a socio-political and moral level, the play is a "plea for marginality," primarily socio-sexual, and by extension, political — according to the author.[9] Serge expresses this plea eloquently in a speech to Lucienne:

J'me sacre de ce que le reste du monde peut penser, nous autres on est heureux, pis c'qu'on ressent l'un pour l'autre, si c'est une maladie, c'est une maudite belle maladie! Que personne vienne me dire j'ai pas le droit! J'ai le droit d'être heureux comme tout le monde. . . . respectez-nous donc, nous autres, on est heureux! (91) (I don't give a damn what the rest of the world thinks, we're happy, the two of us, and if what we feel for each other is sick, well, then it's a goddamn beautiful disease! Let no one come to tell me I'm not allowed! I have the right to be happy like everybody else. . . . you better show us some respect — we two, we are happy!)

On a universal level, the play deals with the difficulties experienced by human beings in expressing the emotions they feel for each other. Its ultimate message, surprisingly positive and traditional — *amor vincit omnia* — is sufficiently modified by the unorthodox nature of the love portrayed to fit without difficulty into the total Tremblay opus.

Love, as we have seen, is an important element in *Bonjour, là, bonjour,* and faint traces of the same theme appear in *En pièces détachées.* But in *A toi, pour toujours, ta Marie-Lou,* the emotional desert is total and unrelieved. The author considers this work his best play, and from the point of view of technical perfection, he appears to be right. The play is conceived as a "string quartet of four voices."

Although the dialogue of this play appears confusing to the uninitiated reader, *A toi, pour toujours, ta Marie-Lou* exhibits in its construction all the classical qualities of simplicity, harmony and logic. Its form can be reduced to a mathematical formula which consists of five sets of two parallel dialogues (A and B) that come together four times:

A (Marie-Louise and Léopold)   B (Carmen and Manon)

AB

A . . . . B

AB

A . . . . B

AB

A . . . . B

AB

A . . . . B

The play seems confused because the speeches of the four characters in the two dialogues are interwoven (for example, Marie-Louise/Carmen/Léopold/Manon rather than Marie-Louise/Léopold; Carmen/Manon) and also because the author assumes certain conventions of time and place. However, in performance, *A toi, pour toujours, ta Marie-Lou* is a remarkably potent play. Its power derives in part from the concentration provided by the one-act form, which means that the action is uninterrupted. The tragic impact is reinforced by basic adherence to the unities of time and place, but realistic and theatrical elements also intermingle in the conception of this play. In terms of time, we are asked to assume that the two dialogues which run simultaneously are actually taking place ten years apart: Marie-Louise and Léopold are speaking in 1961, immediately before the "accident"; Carmen and Manon, in 1971, ten years after the fact. But within the context of each dialogue the unity of time remains intact: each conversation takes place over a period of time corresponding in duration to the actual performance time. However, at four points in the course of the play, Carmen and Manon cross the time boundary to step into the parents' time zone, a device which reinforces the central themes and brings out in greater relief the main factors of the traumatic parent-child relationship described.

The setting involves a similar theatrical device. Both conversations take place in the kitchen of the parents' house, which provides unity of place, but again only partially. Carmen and Manon are actually situated in the kitchen, centre stage; Léopold and Marie-Louise remain on either side of the stage within symbolic environments suggestive of their habits (the tavern; the rocking chair in front of the television set). In order to clarify the distinction between naturalistic and theatrical elements, the author suggests in his stage directions that the kitchen set should be realistic but that the sets for Léopold and Marie-Louise should only be impressionistic. The suggested style of acting reinforces the theatricalism of the play still more: the characters do not move and never look at each other. Thus, all dramatic development is achieved through verbal interaction.

The external structure of the play revolves around the central event of the parents' accident/suicide. This event terminates one dialogue (Léopold and Marie-Louise) and motivates the other, creating forward and reverse motion at the same time. The four crucial episodes in which the two sets of characters come together serve to explain why the "action" moves in two directions. Because of its structure, the play as a whole creates a sense of tragic fatality not unlike that evoked by *Oedipus Rex;* here, too, everything has already happened before the action starts, and what we witness is an unravelling of both "before" and "after." In this respect, the skeletal structure of *A toi, pour toujours, ta Marie-Lou* shows a perfect symmetry and parallelism:

1961 SCORE	TIME LEVELS MEET	1971 SCORE
(Léopold and Marie-Louise)		(Carmen and Manon)
Dialogue 1 Quarrels (re coffee, toast, vomiting, nausea); sex issue mentioned only briefly.		*Dialogue* 1 Different reactions of Carmen and Manon: Carmen changed, Manon remains the same.

Children listen in
on parents
fighting (43).

Dialogue 2
Quarrels: domestic
matters, household
money.

Dialogue 2
Carmen tries to wake
Manon from her
dreams of the past,
defends father.

Children listen as
mother announces
new pregnancy
and accuses father
of "rape" (50).

Dialogue 3
Basic traumas re-
vealed: problem of
new baby, Léopold's
work. Marie-Louise
taunts him with mad-
ness in the family.

Dialogue 3
Manon's trauma re-
vealed (saw parents
in sex situation);
Carmen taunts
Manon with idea of
hereditary madness.

Children witness
father's attack of
madness (75).

Dialogue 4
Discussion of court-
ship, marriage;
central problem, sex,
brought out into the
open.

Dialogue 4
Religion and sex.

Children made to
listen to father's
accusations
against mother,
her "sex problem"
(82–86).

Dialogue 5
Open admission of
hatred. Parents leave
for car "ride."

Dialogue 5
Manon admits she is
unable to change.
Carmen leaves;
Manon left alone, in
prayer.

This highly rational structure is the unconscious result of a conscious "composition" of the play on musical principles. As mentioned before, Tremblay looks upon *A toi, pour toujours, ta Marie-Lou* as a "string quartet," with the four voices/instruments following their individual melodies, playing variations on a common theme, separating into solos for special effect and joining into four-piece crescendos to raise the level of emotional intensity. Within the overall structure, the dialogues develop exactly like the parts of a musical composition: one instrument (voice) introduces a theme or melody, then another picks it up, varies it, echoes it and further develops it. The first few lines of the play clearly illustrate how the play's construction is based on musical principles:

MARIE-LOUISE: Demain...

CARMEN: Aïe...

LEOPOLD: Ouais...

MANON: Pis...

This "set" is repeated once more: "demain," "aïe," "ouais," "pis." Then, each instrument (voice, character) develops its original theme further:

MARIE-LOUISE: Demain, faudrait . . .

CARMEN: Aïe, ça fait déjà . . .

LEOPOLD: Oui, j'sais . . .

MANON: Pis on dirait . . .

The next set of lines continues to expand the four original "melodies," and some interaction also begins (Marie-Louise/Léopold):

MARIE-LOUISE: Demain, faudrait aller manger sus ma mère . . .

CARMEN: Aïe, ça fait déjà dix ans . . .

LEOPOLD: Oui, j'sais . . . pis ça m'écoeure . . .

MANON: Pis on dirait que ça s'est passé hier . . .

(37)

(MARIE-LOUISE: Tomorrow we've got to go eat at mother's . . .

CARMEN: Wow, it's already ten years . . .

LEOPOLD: Yeah, I know . . . and it makes me sick . . .

MANON: Still, it feels like yesterday . . .)

These initial lines serve as an effective overture to the play as a whole since they set the main motifs and moods. As the play proceeds, the dialogues develop a parallel structure through alternating counterpoint and repetition of the same motifs. Although each dialogue follows its own argument or "melody," identical themes appear simultaneously in both; for example, in dialogue 3:

MARIE-LOUISE: T'aimerais ça, passer dans'vie sans savoir c'qu'y se passe autour de toé, hein, Léopold?

MANON: Tu peux me dire tout c'que tu veux . . . Ça glisse sus'moé comme sus le dos d'un canard!

(65)

(MARIE-LOUISE: You'd love that, going through life without even knowing what's going on around you, wouldn't you, Léopold?

MANON: You can tell me anything you like . . . It runs off me like water off a duck!)

Or, to give another example from dialogue 4:

LEOPOLD: Tu peux rire de moé tant que tu voudras, tu peux me traiter d'écoeurant, de raté, de fou, tout c'que tu voudras, mais moé j'ai rien qu'un mot à dire pis tu vas arrêter ben raide...

MANON: Toé aussi t'en reviens toujours à ça... Comme si y'avait rien que ça dans le monde...

(82)

(LEOPOLD: You can laugh at me all you want, you can call me disgusting, a failure, mad, anything you like, but all I have to do is say a certain word and it'll stop you in your tracks...

MANON: You, too, you always come back to that... As if there was nothing but that in the world...)

The harmonies achieved by this method of composition stand in ironic contrast to the play's theme; nevertheless, the subject matter is served perfectly by the structure.

Although a highly theatrical play, the language of *A toi, pour toujours, ta Marie-Lou* remains on a realistic/naturalistic level. The tone is set at the very beginning, as Léopold and Marie-Louise mercilessly review each other's bedroom/bathroom activities using a whole list of unsavoury, crude expressions — "renvoyer," "péter," "cracher" ("vomiting," "farting," "spitting") topped off with a liberal sprinkling of "marde" ("shit") and "ta yeule" ("shut up"). In the course of the play, the characters employ with much skill and gusto all seven basic *sacres*, using them both singly and in combinations. The naturalism in the language is reinforced by the use of a number of key words which help to define the characters and their relationships. Just as the term "maudite vie plate" establishes the general atmosphere of *Les Belles-Soeurs*, so the expressions "écoeurant"/"écoeuré" ("disgusting"/"disgusted") run through this play. They are used liberally by every one of the characters except Carmen and indicate both their attitude towards life in general and to others in the family specifically: Marie-Louise finds Léopold "écoeurant"; Léopold in turn is disgusted by his wife; and Manon maintains her particular disgust for her father even ten years after his death.

Other key words that suggest character are "cochon," "cochonne," "cochonnerie" ("swine," "filthy pig") — Marie-Louise's standard reaction to any mention of sex; the terms "machine" and "engrenage" are used by Léopold to describe both the physical realities of his working life and the sense of being caught up in a system of cogwheels from which there is no escape; "dans la lune" ("lost in dreams") is Carmen's diagnosis of her sister's difficulties; "martyre" and "pitié" refer to both Marie-Louise and Manon; and finally, "piquer une crise" ("to throw a fit") is used in connection with both Léopold and Manon.

Irony saturates the play, especially in the dialogue between Marie-Louise and Léopold, and serves to demonstrate the hatred of the characters for each other. When Léopold is at the peak of his anger, he calls his wife "ma chérie, ma belle p'tite Marie-Lou," expressions that evoke the days of their courtship and heighten her present exasperation. Marie-Louise retorts in kind when she calls her husband "mon beau Léopold." She achieves dizzying heights of irony and cynicism in the speech which announces to him her latest pregnancy: "Es-tu content, mon loup, mon chéri, mon beau trésor, on va en avoir un autre! Un autre beau cadeau du ciel! Envoye, grimpe après les murs, pends-toé après les lumières, donne-moé un beau bec sucré! Serre-moé dans tes bras comme dans les vues pis dis-moé: 'Chérie, que je suis heureux!'" (52) ("Are you happy, my tiger, my darling, my beautiful treasure, we're going to have another one! Another beautiful gift from heaven! Go ahead, climb up on the walls, swing from the lamps, give me a big sweet kiss! Hold me in your arms like in the movies and then tell me: 'Darling, how happy I am!'").

Monologue is not as important in this play as in some of the others. However, Tremblay does use the monologue technique several times to give a full account of certain particularly significant events in his characters' lives, events that have shaped their entire outlook on life. Manon has two such monologues: her account of how, as a child, she fought against being likened to her father, and her account of how she found her parents in bed; Léopold has only one monologue (his work experience), and Marie-Louise has one (her mother's inadequate sexual instruction). All together, these linguistic devices combine to create four characters who come fully alive in spite of the fact that there is no stage movement whatsoever.

Of course, it would be totally unfair to both the play and the author to restrict its interpretation to the level of political parable. However, the sociological message is obviously an indictment of the working-class family, its living conditions, taboos, sexual ignorance; finally, *A toi, pour toujours, ta Marie-Lou* also raises the basic question of all great works in the humanistic tradition: how can man live in a world governed by forces largely out of his control, both within and outside himself? Tremblay does not attempt to give an answer, but he does suggest all three options considered by existentialist philosophy: suicide, the way of Léopold and Marie-Louise; a life of bad faith, the case of Manon; and full recognition of the fact of freedom, assumption of that freedom and the moral responsibility that goes with it — Carmen's choice. In an absurd world, she has created meaning and purpose for herself. Seen from this point of view, Carmen becomes a true heroine in the sense of Sartre (*Being and Nothingness*) and Camus (*The Myth of Sisyphus*). The theme is carried further in the next Carmen play, *Sainte Carmen de la Main*.

As Michel Tremblay's pioneering use of *joual* as a dramatic idiom helped to pave the way for his younger contemporaries in the seventies, so did his bold attacks on the traditional myths of family and motherhood. Rejection of the family has become as commonplace a feature of the *jeune théâtre* as has the use of *joual*. Paule Baillargeon, of the company Grand Cirque Ordinaire, summed up the prevailing attitude when she said, "Quelle que soit la forme, c'est 'non' à la famille"[10] ("Whatever the form [of the play], it's 'no' to the family"). Many of the new socio-poetic improvisations of the young companies have the family unit as a target for their satire. Spectacles such as *La Famille transparente* of the Grand Cirque Ordinaire, or *Quand le matricarcat fait des petits,* a production of the théâtre euh!, parallel, in a nonliterary way, the negative view of the family that we find in the work of Michel Tremblay.

CHAPTER FIVE

Debunking a Dream:
Grotesque Love and Monstrous Sexuality

For the character of Carmen in *A toi, pour toujours, ta Marie-Lou,* the Main represents an effective escape from the prison of the family to a more liberated life — though, objectively speaking, she simply exchanges one ghetto for another. In *Trois Petits Tours, Hosanna, La Duchesse de Langeais* and *Demain matin, Montréal m'attend,* Tremblay demonstrates how the lives of those who have thrown off the shackles and taboos of the family can be as great a hell as the *maudite vie plate* of those who have chosen to remain within the bonds of domesticity. Whereas the underlying theme of all the family plays is frustration and desire for escape, the Main cycle deals with the problem of alienation and its complementary search for identity. These themes are explored in the mode of the grotesque, with the transvestite as both the central symbol of alienation and an embodiment of the crisis of identity.

The resulting proliferation of homosexuals and transvestites in the dramaturgy of Tremblay has occasionally caused criticism. It must therefore be emphasized very strongly at this point that we are not dealing with realistic plays, regardless of the sometimes deceptive surface of naturalism. Rather, we should look at these works as parables in which the basic plot or situation is a springboard to other meanings. The symbolism obviously functions on several levels, since alienation can be viewed as a universal problem—the major trauma of modern man—or else more specifically as a disease related especially to Quebec. Tremblay himself is quite outspoken about his reasons for focussing on marginal characters (a predilection he shares with Tennessee Williams): "I am not a realistic playwright. If I choose to talk about the fringes of society, it is because my people are a fringe society."[1]

With alienation as his main theme, and the grotèsque as its mode of expression, Tremblay has moved into the mainstream of contemporary drama, where the grotesque has come to be recognized as the most effective aesthetic technique for rendering in artistic terms the alienation traumas of modern man. "Grotesque" was originally an architectural term, and in that context it connotes an intentional disruption of harmony, a breaking up of the rational order of things, including a blurring of the distinction between human, animal and plant. Transferred to a literary context by Montaigne, the word acquired further connotations of distortion and caricature. Romantic writers were fascinated with the potential of the grotesque mode; it will be useful to remember Victor Hugo's juxtaposition of "grotesque" with its antithesis, "sublime." The nineteenth-century preoccupation with the double or split self looks back to the morality play, in which human nature is divided into forces of good and evil, and forward to the seemingly more sophisticated theories of Freud; the same idea found new forms of expression in the early twentieth century with the Italian *teatro del grottesco* and plays such as Chiarelli's *The Mask and the Face*. From Chiarelli's device of the mask as a symbol of loss of true identity it is but a short step to Tremblay's transvestite disguises and impersonations.

The grotesque mode in drama leads to the modern tragicomedy, a genre that has proven itself capable of conveying the tragic aspect of modern life without falling back on the forms and elevated style of the classical tragedy, which appear incongruous in the twentieth century. The grotesque genre used by Tremblay and his fellow dramatists could be defined as "tragedy rewritten in different terms."[2] In modern tragicomedies, grotesque distortion takes the place of the sublime idealization of traditional tragedy; pathos stands next to ridicule, and more often than not the final tragic impact means existentialist anguish and a sense of the absurd rather than a confrontation with ultimate and absolute realities.

The grotesque, then, could be described as the natural mode of expression in an age of multiple alienation. Standing well within the mainstream of contemporary literature, Tremblay places special emphasis on the universally modern theme of the absence or impossibility of love. We have seen this element already in his treatment of the family. In the transvestite plays, it gains added pathos when we are presented with grotesque distortions of love and sexuality that often appear as painful parodies of the real thing. The extreme example would be the role of the Big Bad Wolf as the main object of sexual attraction in the fairy-tale musical *Les Héros de mon enfance.* Margaret Atwood has suggested that all of Canadian literature suffers from a dearth of normal, healthy sexuality since it abounds in Hecates (Death Goddess/Ice Virgin figures), offers few and usually short-lived Dianas (Maiden figures) and exhibits an almost total absence of Venuses (Love Goddess figures).[3] Tremblay fits into this pattern very well. Certainly, all of the *belles-soeurs* could be classed as Hecates, as could Marie-Louise, Manon, Robertine and Thérèse, not to mention the maiden aunts, Albertine and Charlotte. We find the occasional Diana figure, such as the three young girls in *Les Belles-Soeurs*; but with Venus, a most interesting and suggestive phenomenon appears. The only genuine Venus figures in the entire opus — Carmen and, to a lesser extent, Pierrette of *Les Belles-Soeurs* — are both destroyed by convention. The remainder are but distorted versions of the concept, who either live out their sexual impulses in an incestuous relationship (Nicole) or achieve their status as sex symbol by denying or reversing their real identity (Hosanna, the Duchesse de Langeais). With the last two characters, Tremblay has created universal archetypes of emotional alienation; they obviously exceed the boundaries of any one nation or language.

Tremblay's particular use of the grotesque, however, extends beyond the merely psychological and sexual level to language itself. *Joual*, with its bastardization of classical French and heavy admixture of Americanisms, provides a unique verbal counterpoint to the sexual aberrations that constitute Tremblay's dramatic world with its overtones of cultural alienation. Jacques Lazure's sensitive analysis of the phenomenon links the two dimensions in an unusually positive manner:

Le cerveau du Québec, ses centres nerveux et linguistiques, se tournent particulièrement du côté de la France, tandis que ses instincts de conservation et de sexualité, son dynamisme animal fondé sur sa génétique et sur son écologie l'ancrent solidement dans le terroir nord-américain où il rejoint rapidement les grandes racines proprement américaines. Nul doute que le destin collectif du Québec pivote sur cette ambivalence de structures et d'orientations et se nourrit en définitive de cette alternance de tétées.[4] (The brain of Quebec, her nervous and linguistic centre, tends to turn especially towards France, whereas her instincts of self-preservation and sexuality, her animal dynamism which is based on genetics and ecology anchor her solidly in North American territory, quickly establishing contact with the real American roots. There is no doubt that the collective destiny of Quebec pivots on this ambivalence of structures and orientations and ultimately takes its nourishment from this alternation of feedings.)

Whereas Lazure makes a case for the potentially positive aspect of Quebec's cultural ambivalence, most Québécois writers tend to take the opposite view. Certainly, Tremblay's parables of life on the Main point to a society that is far from healthy. His transvestite characters, with their unceasing desire for further impersonations, clearly reflect a schizophrenic society engaged in an agonized search for its own identity. Just as sexual freedom is a symbol of individual psychological and cultural liberation in the family plays, so the sexual identity crisis here becomes an allegory for the identity crisis of an entire community.

Each one of the plays mentioned in this chapter treats the common theme in a distinctly different manner. The three short pieces that make up the triptych *Trois Petits Tours* provide a behind-the-scenes look at life in a cabaret on the Main. By combining the stories of Berthe, an eminently ordinary, middle-aged ticket lady; Charlotte Toupin (alias Carlotta), a fortyish glamour girl who appears in a trained poodle act; and a would-be superstar, Gloria Star, who never "makes it," Tremblay has structured a composition in three movements on the theme of disillusionment, frustration and lost identity. *Hosanna* centres altogether on an identity crisis: a frustrated Claude-turned-Hosanna-turned-Elizabeth Taylor playing Cleopatra is rudely shocked out of his/her carefully concocted illusions and is forced to take stock of who he/she really is. Analysis of a complex and touching love relationship adds further poignancy to this play. Finally, the two-act monologue, *La Duchesse de Langeais*, features an aging drag queen with a broken heart. This play combines pathos and great psychological insight with a satirical takeoff on the ideal of the sex symbol. The monologue portrays the identity crisis of the character and, by extension, of the group.

In *Demain matin, Montréal m'attend*, the "hideous trophy" which remains conspicuous throughout the play effectively symbolizes the shallowness and vulgarity of Louise Tetrault's aspirations to the glamorous life and the essential fallacy of her attempt to turn into a new and different self, "Lyla Jasmin": "Tu peux sortir la fille de l'est mais pas l'est d'la fille" (49) ("You can take a girl out of East Montreal, but you can't take East Montreal out of the girl") is the realistic/pessimistic leitmotif of this musical comedy.

Looking at the plays in greater detail, we shall see that each in turn serves to debunk the old dream of liberation through escape from family living. The characters are left to cope with a *maudite vie plate* which differs in detail but not in essence from that described in *Les Belle-Soeurs*.

Trois Petits Tours is a symphony of alienation in three movements, with frustration as its leitmotif. A steady alternation between illusion and reality provides the counterpoint. The triptych grows in scope and complexity, from the simplicity of *Berthe* (a one-character monologue), to the *théâtre-vérité* style of dialogue between the two characters in *Johnny Mangano and His Astonishing Dogs*, and climaxing in the centrifugal and absurdist *Gloria Star*, which has numerous characters. In keeping with the extension of the theme, the rhythms of the three playlets also become successively stronger. They build in intensity from Berthe's slow shifts between her real life and her dream world, to Carlotta's insistent hammering home of the facts of life to a defensive Johnny, and finally to the frantic climax of torrential outpourings from the lady agent in the last play.

Berthe has spent her life in the ticket booth of the Coconut Inn cabaret. Her tone of profound hopelessness and frustration finds its physical equivalent in the central image of the cage. Imprisoned in her cage of glass, Berthe lives a life of endless routine, of boredom without relief. She cannot even see the shows to which she sells tickets. Corresponding to the sense of imprisonment inherent in the cage image is the thrice-repeated refrain, "Jusqu'à quand, mon Dieu, jusqu'à quand?" ("How much longer, Lord, how much longer?"), an ironic allusion to the *Confessions of St. Augustine.* Berthe is well over forty and quite aware that life has passed her by without offering a chance for reprieve, and so she seeks refuge in long sequences of daydreaming, obviously inspired by the movie magazines she reads. In the dream sequences, she endlessly reconstructs her life in images of glamour and success. Throughout the entire playlet dream and reality alternate, and the excursions into a "better" life are introduced by a change in language, from slang to a more correct syntax and a more elaborate vocabulary. However, the dreams of adventure and the high life, complete with evening dress and champagne, are invariably interrupted by the doorman's cries of "showtime!" which bring Berthe back to reality. Her speech ends in a finale of existentialist despair as she contemplates the facts of her existence: "C'est tellement long! C'est tellement long. Pis c'est tellement plate!" (17) ("It just goes on and on. And it's so boring!").

Johnny Mangano and His Astonishing Dogs (the original title is in English, another reminder of the alienation theme) takes us a step further into the life of the cabaret, from the ticket window to one of the dressing rooms. This turns out to be just another kind of cage, and a lot less clean than the glass enclosure that houses Berthe. The dressing room provides temporary headquarters for Johnny and his retinue: seven or eight dogs "of every conceivable breed," a monkey, and his partner Carlotta. In a much more dramatic way than *Berthe, Johnny Mangano* deals with the same problems of disappointment, the discrepancy between dream/illusion and reality, and the impossibility of changing an unbearable situation. The themes of alienation and lost identity are especially accentuated in this play.

There is some slight story line in *Johnny Mangano*, but on the whole, as with the plays of Beckett, the events shown on stage do not seem to represent a single, unique action, but rather one isolated example from a routine that is bound to go on and on.

The action centres on Carlotta. At the age of forty, she looks back on a lifetime spent on stage behind Johnny and his trained dogs, her lovely legs and provocative costume catering to the prurient interests of those members of the audience who might find an animal act less than exciting. In spite of Johnny's almost professional capacity for self-deception and the creation of illusions all around, Carlotta has moments of lucidity when she fully realizes that she has given up her life, her very being, for the sake of an "artistic" endeavour which has never amounted to anything, and never will. The play shows us Carlotta in just such a moment of lucid self-appraisal as she confronts Johnny and forces him to accept the evident truth about himself and his act. She announces that she has decided to leave before the start of the second show of the evening. Suspense builds up; showtime is only minutes, then seconds, away. Johnny's initial cocky self-confidence gives way to panic as Carlotta shows no intention of relenting. Eventually, while the master of ceremonies is heard ad-libbing in a desperate attempt to gain time, Johnny humbles himself, falls on his knees and admits he cannot go on without her. This is an argument Carlotta cannot resist. Grabbing Kiki, the old apricot poodle she detests, she rushes out into the spotlights once more, ready to carry on, regardless: "Viens, ma belle Kiki, viens dans tes beaux spots roses, ma tante va faire la folle, pendant ce temps-là, en arrière de toi..." (46) ("Come on, Kiki, my beauty, come to your lovely pink spotlights, meanwhile auntie will make a fool of herself behind you . . . "). Carlotta's use of the third person in referring to herself here serves to underline further her sense of alienation.

The confrontation between Johnny and Carlotta reiterates the age-old arguments of the battle of the sexes, arguments which we find, in various forms, in our literary tradition since the Greeks. Carlotta taunts Johnny with the fact that she has given up everything—her family and a secure life—for his sake; indeed, she points out, whatever professional success he has had, he owes to her. Johnny does not try to deny Carlotta's essential contributions to their act. This, however, is not the point. His real defence lies in the fact that Carlotta followed him of her own free will, because she was in love; and if she stays, it is because she cannot live without him. The arguments on both sides are essentially the same as the ones in that archetypal confrontation between Jason and Medea, as presented by Euripides. They raise disquieting questions about the true nature of love and the part played within that most noble of emotions by the ignoble instinct which Brecht refers to in his famous ballad as "sexuelle Hoerigkeit," the tyranny of sex.

These considerations are not, however, thematically central to the play; they only provide a psychological foundation for the main themes. These themes include, first of all, the hopelessness of Carlotta's situation: in spite of her momentary rebellion, she knows very well that there is no way out for her, any more than there is for Berthe. In fact, Berthe's final words, quoted earlier, could serve as an introduction to *Johnny Mangano*.

Johnny has managed to live with the frustrations and failures of his own life, simply because he is a veritable wizard at creating illusion. This capacity is symbolized by the fanciful array of coloured spotlights he has dreamt up for his show. Not unexpectedly, he protests vehemently when Carlotta tries to awaken him from his technicolour dream; however, she will not give up. Eventually, he is forced to accept the facts as she mercilessly exposes the realities of their "art": "Aïe, veux-tu que j'te dise que c'est que ça vaut, not'numéro, Johnny, veux-tu que j'te dise que c'est que ça vaut? C'est effrayant, not'numéro, Johnny, c'est ridicule!" (35) ("Hey, do you want me to tell you what our act is worth, Johnny, do you want me to tell you? It's plain ghastly, our act, and what's more, it's ridiculous!"). This realization reduces both performers' lives to a zero point of failure and utter meaninglessness. For Carlotta, there is the added trauma of identity loss. She no longer knows who she is, because she has for so long played the role of a mere stage prop. In her moment of revolt, she desperately clings to the sense of identity and security connected with her "real" name and pleads with Johnny not to call her Carlotta when they are by themselves: "J'm'appelle Charlotte, Johnny! Charlotte Toupin! C'est ben laid, mais que c'est que tu veux, c'est mon nom! Mon vrai! pis j'y tiens!" (27-28) ("My name is Charlotte, Johnny! Charlotte Toupin! So what if it's ugly, it's my name! My real one! And it means something to me!").

The costume she is obliged to wear further emphasizes the role-playing aspect of her life, in which the "real" Charlotte Toupin has become lost. Carlotta's array does not allow for the expression of individuality; she appears in the classical outfit of her profession: hair dyed to a platinum blonde, extra heavy make-up, clinging gold lamé trimmed with ostrich feathers. But Johnny can see nothing wrong with her apparel, except perhaps that it has become somewhat shabby and timeworn (the dogs' costumes have had priority); neither is he particularly shocked when she points out to him that his own costume is an exact replica of the monkey's. But Carlotta is fully aware that her part in the act has robbed her of a sense of identity: "Ça fait douze ans que je fais la 'girlie' sur le stage en arrière de tes chiens, que je montre mes cuisses au monde pour qu'y applaudissent plus fort, tu trouves pas ça tordant?" (33) ("For twelve years now I've been playing the 'girlie' on the stage behind your dogs, I show my thighs to the public to make them clap harder, don't you think it's a scream?"). Her humiliation becomes complete at the end of the act, when the dogs exit in a blaze of light, while she must grope her way backstage as best she can in total darkness.

The animal act itself reinforces Carlotta's sense of alienation. The monkey pops out from his box dressed as Uncle Sam and waves an American flag; the star of the show, the old trouper Kiki, is a truly grotesque caricature—a fat old poodle dressed up as a young bride. When Carlotta protests that this spectacle makes her feel "sick to her stomach," she is simply experiencing the "nauseous quality of life," as Sartre has put it in somewhat more sophisticated terms. In the thematic context of the Tremblay dramaturgy, the grotesquely outfitted animals and their trainers serve exactly the same symbolic purpose as the transvestites—an illustration of alienation and loss of identity.

Part three of the triptych, *Gloria Star*, carries the theme of pathetic fantasy to its logical conclusion: the superstar who is the embodiment of everyone's dreams never appears, and the play ends on an absurdist note tinged with satire. Technically, this play completes the ever-expanding structure of the trilogy: from the single character of the first monologue and the two protagonists of *Johnny Mangano* we now move to a full complement of characters: Carlotta and the girls of the chorus line backstage, ready to make their entrance; the director; and a mysterious woman who introduces herself as the agent of Gloria Star, the striptease queen.

Although this third play in the trilogy is somewhat diffuse in both theme and structure, the central idea comes across very well. Having announced the arrival of Gloria Star and checked on all the spectacular arrangements for her act, the agent suddenly appears to go mad. She offers to take the (male) director in hand and present him as the greatest striptease act ever. As the agent single-mindedly pursues this weird obsession, the director tries to give instructions to his lighting engineer for the current act, prepare for the next, and simultaneously fight off the insistent advances of the maniacal woman. This scene is straight out of the Theatre of the Absurd, but it nonetheless carries very serious overtones. The agent, like many Tremblay characters, is in pursuit of an impossible dream: she wants to achieve the ultimate, an absolute standard of physical perfection. Gloria Star was to have been her apogee. Following her inevitable disappointment when the "star" fails to appear, her quest for an absolute becomes grotesque, for she suddenly discovers a new idea of perfection: she conceives of a male striptease act which will usher in the era of men as sex objects. Her eloquence reaches its peak as she proclaims the glories of the human body, only to be silenced by an exasperated director.

Unlike the two preceding short pieces, which remain on a naturalistic level, this play ends on a surrealistic note, with a sudden blackout and the appearance of a mysterious female figure. This figure spirits away all the characters except the director, who follows her dance steps in a hypnotic trance. In spite of its obvious weaknesses, *Gloria Star* does carry the themes of the entire triptych to their logical conclusion, which is necessarily absurd. One could hardly think of a more forceful image for debunking unrealistic dreams of glamour and fame than the nonappearance of the great Gloria Star. Tremblay, as usual, offers no escape; but in this last play, he treats himself, and the audience, to the pseudoescape of a completely fantastic conclusion.

Hosanna, a full-length play, is clearly superior to the three short pieces that make up *Trois Petits Tours*, both as a political/cultural parable and as a play of psychological analysis. As a parable, it uses the device of the transvestite, Claude/Hosanna, as a multilevel symbol of collective alienation. On the level of psychological analysis, it offers a gripping insight into the complex workings of a lovers' relationship, in which the fact that both happen to be male becomes irrelevant.

Tremblay follows Racine's method of classical concentration by presenting his central character in a moment of crisis; there is no physical action or plot line. The play rigorously observes the classical unities: the setting is the bachelor apartment shared by Hosanna and her lover/husband, Cuirette (Leatherjacket); and the dramatic action covers a time span of no more than a few hours, late one Hallowe'en night.

As the dialogue progresses, we gradually learn what has happened to disturb the relationship between the lovers. The annual Hallowe'en party at Sandra's transvestite club had given Hosanna a chance to realize her life's dream, to act the part of Elizabeth Taylor in the role of Cleopatra. However, it turns out that the other regulars of the club resent Hosanna and had decided to teach her a lesson. When she made her grand entrance at the party, she found everyone in the room dressed exactly as she was. Her discomfiture was greeted with riotous laughter; even Cuirette could not help joining in. Thoroughly humiliated, Hosanna fled to the safety of her home; she was deeply wounded by what she considered Cuirette's "treason."

Her mood is matched by the desolate atmosphere of her apartment, whose appearance Tremblay has indicated carefully in his stage directions. The single room is divided by a counter into a kitchenette on one side and a combination dining-living-bedroom on the other. The decor speaks of monotony, poverty and bad taste, with its uniform shades of brown and hideous furnishings. The few personal items eloquently testify to the tenants' uprooted lifestyle: the radio, record player and television set are all portable. Only two objects in this room clearly reflect the personality of the inhabitants: the large "erotic" painting which hangs, unframed, over the sofa bed, pathetic testimony to Cuirette's ambitious beginnings as an artist; and the dressing table, covered with jars, bottles and cosmetic implements of every description, the all-important place where Claude effects his nightly transformation into Hosanna. In order to keep the transvestite theme before the audience at all times, the author even stipulates that the smell of Hosanna's penetrating perfume (a cause of constant irritation to Cuirette) should be noticeable throughout the performance. In front of the window, the neon light advertising the pharmacy across the street flashes off and on throughout the play — an ambiguous detail open to multiple symbolic interpretations.

The confrontation between the humiliated Hosanna and a half-guilty, half-aggressive Cuirette is developed in a two-act sequence. This division of what is essentially one consecutive dialogue into two parts is designed to illustrate the progressive stages of awareness of the central character, Hosanna. Act I shows us Hosanna immediately upon her return from the disastrous Hallowe'en party, but, throughout the act, she carefully avoids any reference to the painful event. Instead, we are given an insight into the petty irritations, disappointments and strong, if ambiguous, feelings that characterize the relationship between Hosanna and her lover. In the second act, Hosanna finally progresses to some serious soul-searching, and arrives at a number of important insights about herself; she is at last able to verbalize her feelings about the party as she learns to accept her real identity. There is thus a clear line of evolution from beginning to end of the play. However, this evolution might have been shown just as well, perhaps better, in a shorter work containing no interruption.

The element of musical structure, evident in most Tremblay plays, is apparent in *Hosanna* especially in the highly elaborate alternation between monologue and dialogue, and in the orchestration of these speeches. This is particularly true of the second act. Act 1 is organized relatively simply: it starts with a monologue by Hosanna (12-14), but soon switches to dialogue between the two characters, a dialogue that reflects surface interaction but an essential lack of communication. Act 2 begins with a long "solo," a monologue by Hosanna (55-67). This is followed by a section of dialogue between Hosanna and Cuirette; however, the dialogue really consists of two independent, interwoven monologues with no connecting points. This recitative then becomes a "duet" as the two characters speak simultaneously (70-71); but the duet is discordant rather than harmonious, since each character recites different lines. Hosanna's final solo (monologue), delivered to the accompaniment of an understanding Cuirette's hands on her shoulders, clears the air for communication, and the play ends with the final duet in which Cuirette and Hosanna establish genuine dialogue.

Because *Hosanna* is essentially a psychological drama, it uses few theatrical elements; instead there is a straightforward progression and development of the psychological theme. However, the realistic psychology of the play is somewhat strained by the choice of characters (a male transvestite and his/her lover), by the bizarre quality of the situation (a transvestites' Hallowe'en party), and by a certain element of grotesque caricature of Hosanna's and Cuirette's appearance. These elements seem to support the political parable of the play rather than its universal psychological theme.

The main interest of the play, however, remains its presentation of characters in conflict. Both Hosanna and Cuirette are extremely pathetic—Cuirette somewhat less so than

Hosanna since his psychological make-up is considerably simpler. Cuirette is the typical ex-jock, who has difficulties buttoning his once-sexy leather jacket over his increasingly bulging middle, but who has lost none of the arrogant self-assurance of his better days. Only in rare moments of insight will he admit the fact of his decline: "Chus pus c'que j'étais. Bon. Okay. Chus plus gros... J'ai d'la misère à embarquer dans mes culottes pis j'ai pas d'argent pour m'en acheter d'autres... Okay. J'parle plus fort qu'avant pour faire semblant que ça ne me fait rien..." (43) ("I'm no longer what I used to be. Fine. Okay. I am getting fat... I have trouble squeezing into my pants and I don't have money to buy a new pair... Okay. So I talk louder than before to pretend I don't care..."). Cuirette's chagrin is due not only to his declining sex appeal, but also to his failure as an artist. Although he denies it vehemently, Hosanna's assertion that Cuirette takes dope to escape from his frustrations is obviously correct. As the "man in the family," then, Cuirette follows pretty much the pattern of impotent males we have found in the family plays — he belongs to the clan of the Léopolds and Gérards.

Hosanna, on the other hand, is a much more complex character than any of Tremblay's wife or mother types. Her first appearance on stage is calculated to create an emotional reaction that will influence the audience for the rest of the play. The author has given minute stage directions to ensure the desired result:

Hosanna est un travesti habillé comme Elisabeth Taylor dans «Cléopâtre,» en infiniment plus cheap, évidemment. Une Cléopâtre-de-la-Main. Sa robe est en dentelle rouge vin... La perruque est en «cheveux véritables»... l'amoncellement de bijoux, de colliers, de bracelets, de chaînes, de bagues, d'épinglettes... et les serpents qui s'enroulent autour des bras de Cléopâtre-Hosanna proviennent de tous les quinze cents... entre Amherst et Saint-Laurent, sur la Catherine... Mais malgré ce déguisement grotesque, Claude-Hosanna-Cléopâtre ne doit pas être «drôle.» C'est un travesti cheap avec tout ce que ça comporte de touchant, de triste, d'exaspérant et d'exaltant parce qu'exalté. (12–13) (Hosanna is a transvestite dressed like Elizabeth Taylor in *Cleopatra*, only infinitely more "cheap," of course. A Cleopatra-of-the-Main. Her dress is of wine-red lace . . . The wig made of "real hair" . . . the accumulation of jewels, collars, bracelets, chains, rings, pins . . . and the serpents which encircle the arms of Cleopatra-Hosanna come from every five-and-ten along St. Catherine Street . . . between Amherst and St. Laurent . . . but in spite of this grotesque disguise, Claude-Hosanna-Cleopatra must not appear "funny." She is a cheap transvestite, touching and sad, exasperating and exalting, because she is exalted.)

Throughout the first act Hosanna inspires pathos, her actions ranging from the near ridiculous (her futile attempts to wriggle out of her dress) to the almost sublime (when she orders Cuirette off to Sandra's party in spite of her agonizing jealousy). The pathos reaches an emotional high point in Hosanna's revelations about her relationship with her mother, and the ignoble role which the latter played in pushing Claude, as a young boy, into his (her) present way of living because she thought it would be an excellent way of keeping her son with her always.

In the second act, Hosanna comes to terms with the experience she has just lived through. In a demonstration of courage in the face of adversity ("the show must go on"), she proceeds to probe into the hidden motivations for her obsession with the role of Cleopatra. At this point the character assumes universal significance, as we discover that Hosanna's desire to "be" Elizabeth Taylor–Cleopatra is her personal version of the quest for transcendence, in the full metaphysical sense of that word. She even uses religious terminology to describe her aspirations. For twenty years she has dreamt of impersonating her idol, but did not feel "worthy." When the moment comes, she goes through a purification ritual which leaves her more than clean: "Une matière vierge! J'me sentais comme une statue de la sainte du même nom!" (63) ("Virgin matter! I felt like a statue of the Virgin Mary!"). Hosanna remains a pathetic figure because she fails in her quest, yet at this point her pathos assumes a universal dimension.

Through probing into her own compulsions and motivations, Hosanna manages to come to terms with Cuirette at the end of the play. Their dialogue is a continuous circle of direct and indirect accusations and justifications in which every nuance of their love-hate relationship comes under scrutiny.

Each act can be viewed as a round in an emotional boxing match: both rounds end with an affirmation of love, the first inconclusive, the second final. Like the protagonists themselves, the love relationship is essentially pathetic and long past its prime. Cuirette's and Hosanna's sexual attraction for each other is greatly diminished, having been eroded by infidelity and jealousy, but their relationship seems nonetheless highly charged emotionally. They exchange insults, viciously accuse each other, and even become violent: Hosanna crushes a burning cigarette in Cuirette's face and he retaliates with a brutal blow. As with Léopold and Marie-Louise, the climax of the battle occurs when the question of sex is finally brought out into the open. Hosanna cynically denies feeling any passion ("what we do now is strictly therapeutic"), but Cuirette, hurt to the quick, thinks he can force her to admit that his lovemaking still gives her considerable pleasure. The first round of the battle ends inconclusively — as it must, since they have not discussed the central issue, the injury done to Hosanna at the club. Cuirette manages to scream "I love you, dammit" at Hosanna just before he rushes out of the room, presumably to join Sandra and her gang. When he returns some time later, Hosanna has gone through a great deal of introspection. She is calmer now, and so is Cuirette, having spent his time at the Parc Lafontaine rather than at Sandra's. Although their talk remains at cross-purposes most of the time, at least they are both capable of facing the issue. Finally, they achieve a brief moment of genuine communication. Hosanna now feels free to renounce her disguise — Cleopatra or whatever; and Cuirette is ready to accept her for what she is: "L'important, c'est que tu soyes toé. C'est tout... Claude... c'est pas Hosanna que j'aime... Va te démaquiller... " (75) ("What counts is that you're you. That's all... Claude... it's not Hosanna that I love.... Go take off your make-up...". Hosanna removes her slip, and the play ends with Cuirette taking Claude's naked male body in his arms.

As this brief summary of the psychological theme in *Hosanna* clearly shows, the problem of identity is central to the play. Hosanna represents alienated man in search of an identity. Her attempts to "build" a personality from the outside illustrate exactly what Pirandello meant by his concept of *cos-truirsi*—the "construction" of one or many personalities, as the need arises, to compensate for the absence of a solid, stable, "absolute" identity. For Hosanna, this construction process follows a pattern of concentric circles that move outward from the centre, starting with the name change from the masculine and everyday "Claude" to the feminine and exalted "Hosanna," proceeding through changes in physical appearance by the use of the entire transvestite armamentarium of make-up, wigs, feminine clothing and perfume, and finally ending in elaborate role playing which distances the character farther and farther from the core of his original personality: from Claude to Hosanna to Elizabeth Taylor, to Elizabeth Taylor as Cleopatra.

The farther the character gets from the core he has abandoned, the more he is afraid to look back: Hosanna cries when she faces the mirror, refuses to remove her make-up, and clings to the security of her wig even when it is time to go to bed. However, she is too intelligent not to realize that she is practising self-deception. When her emotional resistance breaks down in the course of her confrontation with Cuirette, she eventually reveals the painful and pathetic crisis of identity which underlies her life: "Chus ridicule quand chus déguisé en homme... Pis chus ridicule quand chus déguisée en femme ... Pis chus t'encore plus ridicule quand chus poignée comme ça, entre les deux, avec ma tête de femme, mes sous-vêtements de femme, pis mon corps... " (29) ("I'm ridiculous when I'm disguised as a man... And I'm ridiculous when I'm disguised as a woman... And I'm even more ridiculous when I'm caught like that, between the two, with my head like a woman's, my underwear like a woman's and my body... ").

As she recapitulates the events of the evening, she realizes that the structure she has so painstakingly built up in pursuit of her dream identity has been smashed to bits, has collapsed like a house of cards: "Vous avez toute démoli ma vie en papier mâché" (74) ("You've fully demolished my papier-mâché life"). Once she has accepted the fake quality of her life, the conclusion is inevitable: "Chus t'un homme, Cuirette!" ("Cuirette, I'm a man!"). When Cuirette accepts the fact, Hosanna can at last drop all pretense; and in her last speech of the play, she addresses her lover by his real name, Raymond: "R'garde, Raymond, chus t'un homme! Chus t'un homme, Raymond! Chus t'un homme!" (75) ("Look, Raymond, I'm a man! I'm a man, Raymond! I'm a man!").

For Raymond/Cuirette, there is a corresponding, if less striking, image of disalienation: his discovery that the Parc Lafontaine, site of the sexual activities of his youth, has lost all its appeal since the city has chosen to light up even its remotest corners with electric lamps. For Cuirette, as for Hosanna, it is the end of an era: "Cleopatra is dead, and the Parc Lafontaine is all lit up" (75). Both characters realize that the time for hiding places and disguises is past and they must assume real life and real identities.

As mentioned before, *Hosanna* can be interpreted on three levels: as a psychological drama dealing with interpersonal relationships; as a philosophical play dealing with the problem of identity; and as a political parable. Tremblay himself insists on the political aspect of the play: "Hosanna deals in a symbolic way with the problems of Quebec... it is an allegory about Quebec. In the end they drop their poses and embrace their real identity.... He kills all the ghosts around him as Quebec did."[5] Perhaps because of its special relevance to a national problem, the play has been eminently successful in both English and French Canada, but less so in New York. However, *Hosanna* will doubtless survive its political uses because its psychological and philosophical themes have universal implications.

In *La Duchesse de Langeais*, Tremblay has achieved a tour de force of a rare kind, if not unique, in dramatic literature: a two-act play consisting entirely of monologues by one character. Tremblay apparently has a particular fondness for the monologue technique, which is based partly on his admiration for Shakespeare. We might also look to Beckett for parallels since Tremblay is a great admirer of his work, in which "dialogue" often consists of a combination of independent monologues. In *Krapp's Last Tape*, in fact, Beckett has done exactly what Tremblay attempts in *La Duchesse de Langeais*: he has created a character whose life is reconstructed on the basis of a single long monologue.

Notwithstanding the obvious pitfalls involved in such a genre, Tremblay's monologue is a brilliant, lively composition, which provides a variety of points of view through the attitudes of the protagonist himself, who constantly shifts back and forth between different levels of sincerity, role playing and more or less conscious self-deception. In fact, Tremblay's aging drag queen might well be the most successful of his entire gallery of dramatic characters. The play is set on the terrace of a café "somewhere down south." It is just after noon, and exceedingly hot. Everyone has left for the obligatory siesta, so that we find the Duchesse alone under the blazing sun. Obviously, this setting is calculated to underline the loneliness and isolation of the character.

In his stage directions concerning the physical appearance of the Duchesse, Tremblay emphasizes the need for balance between the monstrous and the pathetic: "La caricature doit être parfaite, complète, et touchante" (81) ("The caricature must be perfect, complete, and moving"). As the play opens, we find her in a thoughtful pose in front of a half-empty whisky bottle, dressed in "horrible," powder blue American-style leisure clothes. For the second act, she appears in an all-white outfit, which shifts the emphasis from the grotesque to the pathetic, in keeping with her deepening self-analysis and subsequent self-revelations.

Like *Hosanna, La Duchesse de Langeais* functions both as psychological drama and as an exploration of the theme of alienation, on both the personal and the political levels. In terms of human interest, the play deals with the problems of aging; in particular, the humiliation of a "woman" who has been deserted for a much younger partner. In this respect, the fact that the Duchesse is a male transvestite appears merely incidental; any woman of sixty, abandoned after a brief affair with a nineteen-year-old, would react in the same manner. For the Duchesse, the case is somewhat more complicated because it involves her professional pride. As a prostitute of international repute and forty years' standing, she considers it shameful to have allowed herself the unprofessional weakness of falling in love.

The first line of the play, "Ce soir, on ne fait pas l'amour, on se saoûle!" (82) ("Tonight, we don't make love, we get smashed!"), serves as the play's leitmotif, which is repeated at intervals throughout like a refrain. However, as in *Hosanna,* it takes the Duchesse all of act 1 (and in her case also a whole bottle of whisky) to get to the point where she drops her evasion tactics and faces the facts of her unhappy love affair. Meanwhile, she delivers a running commentary on her present and past situation, reminiscing about lovers and adventures in bygone days. Quite obviously, many of her glorious escapades and glamorous anecdotes are pure figments of her imagination. Like Berthe in *Trois Petits Tours*, she constructs for herself the kind of past she would have liked to have had complete with furs, jewels and limousines. As with Berthe, Tremblay draws a linguistic line of demarcation between her dream world, described in highly "refined" language — a caricature of classical French — and her life, which she describes in unabashed *joual.* The mixture of the grotesque, ridicule and pathos which constitutes the Duchesse is thus expressed very forcefully on the linguistic level.

Starting from the more immediately obvious characteristics and working inward towards the subtler elements of the Duchesse's psychology, let us see how the author has managed his verbal character-building. The realistic element which is very strong in the language used by the Duchesse is subtle counterpoint to her name, connoting aristocratic refinement! This particular duchess peppers her speech with scatological references: words like "marde," "queue," "suceuses de cul" ("shit," "tail," "ass-sucker") flow from her mouth as naturally and spontaneously as do the customary *sacres,* "tabarnac," "crisse," "calice," etc.

The Duchesse is also blessed with a magnificently off-colour sense of humour. Her monologue is lively and interesting throughout because of her knack for picturesque expressions and clever turns of phrase. Here, again, the context reflects the Duchesse's occupational background, either directly or indirectly through the choice of imagery. She never allows her professional interests to slip her mind for long: "Envoye, encore un p'tit verre, ma chérie, pis ensuite on va aller cruiser un peu, voir si y'aurait pas quequ'gibier dans les sous-bois" (84) ("Go ahead, one more little glass, my darling, and then we'll go cruising a bit, to check if there isn't some game hiding in the underbrush, maybe"). Her speech is as imagistic as poetry, even though the imagery tends towards the scatological. Turning her grief over the loss of her young lover into ridicule, she says, "Allez dire ça au pompiers, y vont vous pisser dessus!" (88) ("Go tell that to the firemen, they'll piss on it for you!"). Another good example of picturesque language is this description of herself at her first communion: "J'étais une première communiante affreuse . . . tannante comme sept, laide comme un cul de singe gratté à deux mains, le brassard de travers . . . " (98) ("I was an awful first communion child . . . unbearable as they come, ugly like a monkey's ass scratched with two hands, my armband all crooked . . . ").

The basic vulgarity of the character is counterbalanced by a number of consciously assumed woman-of-the-world poses. The Duchesse never lets herself go. Throughout her monologue, she is always acting and addressing each one of her speeches to an imaginary audience. Sometimes, she addresses her colleagues in the profession ("les filles," "mes p'tites filles"); other times, the public or potential clients ("mes trésors-chéris," "mes agneaux"). Even when she is speaking to herself, she keeps up a formal pose, addressing herself, depending on the mood of the moment, as "ma tite-fille," "ma noire," "ma chérie," "duchesse," "ma vieille."

This kind of role playing reveals the essential pathos of the character. There is a painful contrast between her life as it is and her life as she would like it to be; and the Duchesse is fully aware of this contrast. However, she faces her situation with unusual courage and moral stamina. Whenever she speaks about her life, she does it in a way that makes the audience realize that what she leaves unsaid is as important, or more so, than what she says. There is dramatic irony here, but dramatic irony with a twist: the Duchesse is creating a role for herself, though she remains aware that it is only a role.

Two speeches will illustrate the point. Towards the end of act I, she sums up her recollection of the past, including all the ups and downs of her career. There is an aggressively optimistic tone about her speech, but we remain fully conscious of the underlying anguish and despair:

C'que j'ai fait, j'l'ai fait parce que j'voulais le faire!...J'ai fourré sur quatre continents, moi, vous savez!...Oui, quatre continents! J'en ai vu de toutes les couleurs, pis de toutes les *size,* if you know what I mean...Mais c'est parce que j'aimais ça! Mon métier, je l'ai choisi! Pis, j'ai passé une maudite belle vie! D'accord, aujourd'hui, je paye la plupart du temps pour fourrer, mais ça fait pas longtemps!...Oui, mes chéries, la duchesse, c'est quelqu'un! Pis a l'a rien à regretter. Ou presque. (94) (What I did, I did because I wanted to!...I've screwed on four continents, you know!...I've seen them in all colours and sizes, if you know what I mean...But that's because I liked it! I chose my profession! And I've had a goddamn beautiful life! Okay, today I mostly have to pay for a fuck, but that's only been for a short time!...Yes, my dears, the duchess, she's somebody. And she has no regrets. Or almost.)

The two phrases that break up the forced optimism of this speech ("today I mostly have to pay"; "or almost") effectively invalidate everything else being said, so that the speech evokes mainly pity.

The compassion we feel for the aging Duchesse extends beyond her very human suffering. There is additional pathos in the way this particular character tries to come to grips with a broken heart. Her final monologue, at the end of act 2, is a masterpiece of linguistic manipulation, in which the author has managed to reveal all his character's interacting levels of role playing and awareness:

C'est de ta faute! Paye, ma calice, paye! Tu le savais que ça finirait comme ça! Tu le savais!...Ben crève, asteur! Essaie pas de lutter, ça sert à rien! (*Très femme du monde*) On viendra me dire, ensuite, qu'on ne meurt plus d'amour au vingtième siècle!...Lorsequ'on trouvera mon corps...Ben non, ma chérie, on ne meurt plus d'amour par les temps qui courent pis tu le sais bien! Tu mourras pas, c'est ben ça qu'y'est effrayant! Ben oui, c'est correct, t'as d'la peine, là, mais ça va se passer...T'as déjà vu pire! Fini, l'amour, asteur, c'est ben correct...Braille un bon coup, roule un peu sous la table, là, pis après...après, fais comme toujours: dis-toi que t'es la plus belle pis la plus fine, pis que le monde est rempli d'hommes qui t'attendent! ...Les hommes sont à tes pieds, duchesse!...Mais je m'en crisse, j'en veux plus! (105-6) (It's all your fault! Now pay, damn you, pay! You knew it would end like that! You knew it!...Well, then, you can croak now! Don't try to fight it, it won't do any good! (*Very much the lady*) Now let them come and tell me that one doesn't die of a broken heart any longer in the twentieth century!... When they shall come upon my body...Whoa, there, dearie, nobody dies of a broken heart any more and what's more you know it! You're not gonna die, that's the frightening part! Okay, so it's true, it hurts, but it will pass...You've gone through worse! As for love, that's all over with, true...You just have a good cry, roll a bit under the table, there, and then...then, do what you've always done: tell yourself you're the most beautiful, the smartest, and that the world is full of men just waiting for you!...The men are at your feet, duchess! ...Hell, I don't care, I don't want them any longer!)

The tricks of self-deception no longer work. Her defences worn down by alcohol, she collapses against the table, and her final words come as something of a surprise: "On m'appelle la Duchesse de Langeais parce que j'ai toujours rêvé de mourir soeur, Carmélite... En buvant du thé!" (106) ("They call me the Duchesse de Langeais because I've always dreamt of dying as a Carmelite nun... Drinking tea!"). Knowing the author, this final, absurd twist is not hard to explain. His characters often combine attitudes that are polar opposites but are nevertheless derived from one basic mystical or metaphysical aspiration. As becomes obvious from the monologue as a whole, the Duchesse is possessed by a desire for transcendence of some sort, a desire that is manifest in her dreams of impossible feats as an international male courtesan ("I've drunk whisky in every possible/imaginable position"), but could just as well find release in the mystical ecstasies of religious life. We will find this theme more fully elaborated in *Damnée Manon, Sacrée Sandra*.

As in the other plays discussed in this chapter, the theme of alienation in *La Duchesse de Langeais* is heightened through the contrasts between different levels of reality and illusion. This is particularly telling in the case of the Duchesse because she has a large repertoire of fantasy lives. She herself is quite aware of the dizzying confusion of her role-playing game, and understandably proud of her ability to carry it off: "Quand tu peux arriver à faire croire à un homme qu'il couche avec une grande vedette internationale pis que c'te grande vedette féminine-là c'est quand même un homme, parce que c'est avec un homme qu'il veut coucher, ben chapeau!" (89) ("If you can make a man believe that he is going to bed with a great international star, and moreover that this great female star is after all a man, because it's a man he wants to go to bed with, well, hats off!"). The man — playing the Duchesse — playing Galina Oulanova — playing the dying swan — brings us back directly to Claude-Hosanna-Elizabeth Taylor-Cleopatra and the Pirandellian concept of constructing identities. The symbolism obviously applies on a universal level as well. Its application to the Quebec situation is hinted at within the play by the device of the Duchesse's favourite exclamation "aïe, wow, hein," a linguistic troika made up of *québécois,* American and French.

Perhaps better than any of the other plays discussed in this chapter, *La Duchesse de Langeais* answers the description of the modern grotesque tragicomedy. However, the monologue form achieves what few contemporary plays can boast, the creation of a thoroughly convincing and fully human character. Tremblay also succeeds in overcoming our potential resistance to the Duchesse and the grotesque world she represents by skilful manipulation of colourful and entertaining language.

In a lighter vein, but equally effectively, Tremblay's two musicals, *Demain matin, Montréal m'attend* and *Les Héros de mon enfance,* continue the thematology of the Main cycle of plays. In *Demain matin, Montréal m'attend* the action takes place in the pseudorealistic setting of the cabaret, drag bar and bordello we have come to expect, whereas *Les Héros de mon enfance* is set in a fantasy world peopled by the characters from traditional French fairy tales.

It is not surprising that Tremblay, who is exceedingly aware of the large American component in *québécois* culture, should have tried his hand at that most typical of American genres, the musical; but instead of simply imitating the style, he uses it as a base upon which to superimpose his own ideas and techniques. Tremblay's musical comedies share certain essential characteristics of the genre: a lightness of tone, an emphasis on song-and-dance routines, and a fairy-tale atmosphere. However, he refuses to provide the traditional happy ending. Instead of creating an optimistic world based on escape from reality, he shows reality breaking through the façade of make-believe. Thus he turns the genre against itself. Both musicals are heavily satirical, and although they contain a great deal of song, dance, merrymaking and lighthearted gaiety, the effect in the end is pessimistic.

Demain matin, Montréal m'attend deals with the escape from the *maudite vie plate* of family living to the glamour of the cabaret world, and, in so doing, it exposes the tarnished underside of this supposed glamour. The story line is simple: Louise Tetrault, an ordinary little waitress from the village of Saint-Martin, wins a singing trophy in an amateur talent contest and leaves home to become a star in Montreal, where her older sister has already made it "to the top." This would seem to set the scene for the traditional rags-to-riches success story of the conventional musical comedy. Tremblay, however, chooses to ignore the convention and substitutes reality for romantic fantasy. Louise does indeed find her sister, the great "Lola Lee." She also finds that Lola has no intention of sharing her hard-won place at the top with anyone, least of all a kid sister fresh from Saint-Martin. In order to discourage Louise, Lola Lee takes her on a tour of those establishments which will show her what a "show biz" life is really like. This gives the author yet another opportunity to employ his standard images of alienation: backstage at the cabaret; the drag bar; the whorehouse. Even the characters are familiar, for we again meet Hosanna, Cuirette, the Duchesse de Langeais and other regulars of the Tremblay world of prostitutes and transvestites.

Louise is shocked by what she encounters, but not discouraged. Still carrying her trophy at the end of her long night's journey, she remains determined to make a go of a career in show business. The play ends inconclusively, with the surrealistic finale we have come to expect from Tremblay: the two sisters execute a stylized dance which suggests that a fight to the finish is about to take place between them. This is certainly not the happy ending we would expect in a musical, nor is its atmosphere of the idyllic variety that has been associated with the genre since the heyday of Viennese operetta.

On the other hand, *Demain matin, Montréal m'attend* is not a realistic play. The many song-and-dance routines create a level of make-believe; and, as in many of Tremblay's standard dramas, there is a large element of theatricalism that counterbalances the psychological naturalism of certain scenes. In direct contrast to the often spectacular stage settings of musical comedy, *Demain matin, Montréal m'attend* opens on an empty stage, bare except for the "horrible" trophy in the centre. There is no attempt to create realistic settings for any of the environments that Louise visits; as in *Les Belles-Soeurs*, spotlighting is used to single out the groups of characters who carry the action at any given time. The ending is also totally removed from the realm of naturalism, with its stylized choreography and rain of streamers and confetti (reminiscent of the rain of gold bond stamps in *Les Belles-Soeurs*). Incidentally, we find a similar device at the finish of *Les Héros de mon enfance*. Tremblay has an obvious proclivity for ending his plays with an ironic opening up of the heavens.

The structure of *Demain matin, Montréal m'attend* is rather uneven. Act 1 contains five scenes, act 2 only one. The amateur contest in act 1, scene 1 serves as an introduction. In scene 2 Louise is presented with the trophy and decides to leave for Montreal (refrain: "En ville! En ville! En ville!"); scene 3 brings a confrontation between Louise and her mother. The songs here summarize the opposing attitudes of the two characters: Louise's passionate desire to escape from the restrictions of the family ("De l'air! De l'air!"), and the old woman's grief and worry about her children ("Chaque fois que ça sonne à porte..." ["Whenever the doorbell rings..."]). Scene 4 is set in the Bolivar Lounge, the cabaret where Lola Lee stars. We watch Lola Lee and her troupe in action, and the first encounter of the two sisters. They leave together for their tour of Montreal nightlife. Their first stop is the Meat Rack bar (scene 5), a place frequented by transvestites, where Lola Lee points out to an appalled Louise several of the male dancers she found so "sexy" earlier. However, Louise quickly accepts the fact that, as Hosanna explains, "sometimes people are not what they seem" and refuses to be deterred. Act 1 ends with the lamentation of the Duchesse de Langeais, a solo that introduces an elegiac note and recreates the pathos associated with the Duchesse in the earlier play.

Act 2 takes place at Betty Bird's, a bordello where all the girls bear the names of flowers or colours. It is here that Lola Lee made her Montreal debut, as "Marigold." Lola's intention is to get Betty Bird to offer Louise a job and thus frighten her away for good. However, Lola has not counted on the grudge that Betty Bird has harboured against her ever since "Marigold," formerly the star of the establishment, left unceremoniously one day, taking with her Betty's lover Johnny and a portion of the cash. Seeing the possibility of revenge, Betty Bird reveals Lola's little scheme to Louise, and it all comes to naught. The fight for survival of the fittest is on between the two sisters.

Although not a "serious" play, *Demain matin, Montréal m'attend* contains all the central themes of the Tremblay dramaturgy that we have come across earlier. On the family side, there is the *maudite vie plate* motif, with all its concomitants: an ineffectual father who drinks away his life; a mother lost in her martyr complex; and two daughters who cannot wait to escape. This escape leads into themes reminiscent of the Main cycle of plays. Tremblay brutally reveals the underside of the "glamorous" cabaret life: the nightmarish battle for survival and success, which requires a total abdication of pride; the gruelling routine of the "profession" and its more disgusting aspects as seen from backstage; the loneliness, anxiety and insecurity of private lives. The theme of lost identity is brought out through the conventional device of name changes: Rita Tetrault to Lola Lee, alias Marigold; Louise Tetrault to Lyla Jasmin; and the professional names assumed by the whores and transvestites. Alienation and loneliness are everywhere; they find their most complete formulation in the song of the Duchesse which ends act 1. Besides these major themes, the play touches on a number of minor ones: social problems, such as Lola Lee's exploitation of the dancers in the chorus line; human problems related to the position of society's marginal elements; and the "maudit Johnny" theme of male chauvinism, which we are familiar with from *Les Belles-Soeurs*.

In keeping with the tradition of the musical comedy, the characters are not fully developed. Apart from the mother, who has a certain realistic, human appeal, the characters appear as a rather superficial, background chorus to the two protagonists, Louise and Lola Lee. Even the latter do not come across as human beings but rather as operatic puppets going through their paces — which is, of course, appropriate for the genre.

Musical comedy should not be judged exclusively from a literary point of view. Nevertheless, the skilful use of language is an important factor in the genre. In this respect, the play is a definite disappointment: it lacks the linguistic brilliance that we normally expect of Tremblay. The songs seem laboured, as though the author found it difficult to work within the medium of rhyme; and the dialogue lacks that authentic quality which infuses life into a literary character. Perhaps it is Tremblay's failure to find a lingusitic style suitable to the genre that gives this play a somewhat strained, artificial quality. However, given the nature of musical comedy, this weakness might well be concealed by a scintillating production.

Les Héros de mon enfance, on the other hand, represents a rare phenomenon in the history of theatre, a musical comedy that is also a delight to read. The secret of its success lies in its satirical intent, and the skill and apparent ease with which Tremblay handles the satire. *Les Héros de mon enfance* is a light-hearted comedy which was especially written for performance at a summer theatre (Théâtre de la Marjolaine). It employs the full complement of traditional French fairy-tale characters, but they are grotesquely endowed with modern neuroses à la Tremblay, who sets them to performing a mock version of the traditional children's play. The serious underlying theme is cultural alienation; the musical could be described as a mock-heroic, anticolonial protest.

As the author explains in his preface to the play, his own childhood was torn between the rival claims on his imagination of Snow White, Little Red Riding Hood, Cinderella and the rest of the French fairy-tale clan on one side, and Batman, flying saucers and the Walt Disney family on the other; in short, "entre la lointaine et illusoire Europe et la tangible et terre-à-terre Amérique" (7) ("between a far-off and illusory Europe and a tangible and down-to-earth America"). To Tremblay, the traditional French children's stories seem oddly out of place in twentieth-century North America.

By using a mock version of beautiful "français de France" as his linguistic medium, Tremblay subtly denounces cultural ties with Europe. He also uses multiple levels of language with a great deal of panache in this play. For once, he even goes so far as to play games with his audience: "Pour faire plaisir à mes détracteurs, j'ai parsemé mon texte fleuri de mauvaise herbe d'anglicismes. Voyez jusqu'où peut aller la générosité d'un auteur de bonne humeur!" (81) ("To make my detractors happy, I have even gone so far as to spread weeds of anglicisms among my flowery text. You see how far the generosity of an author can go when he is in a good mood!"). The entire play follows this light, bantering tone.

The list of characters contains all the classical heroes from the fairy tales of Charles Perrault: the Wicked Fairy, Little Red Riding Hood, Sleeping Beauty, Cinderella, Tom Thumb, the Big Bad Wolf, etc. However, these characters show distressingly unconventional qualities. Thus, Sleeping Beauty turns out to be a sex maniac; Prince Charming, a homosexual; and innocuous little Tom Thumb, a revolutionary—not to mention the fact that despite the presence of three lovely princesses, the Big Bad Wolf turns out to be the most sexually attractive character in the play. The Wicked Fairy, poor thing, hides the heart of an ordinary bourgeoise under her evil exterior and, what is more, suffers from incurable pangs of love.

This distortion of traditional fairy-tale characters provides the basis for a full-scale satire of both the fairy-tale genre and the children's play. Tremblay satirizes the traditional children's play by allowing the characters to move between different levels of reality, acting and commenting on their actions at the same time. The use of multiple levels of reality also provides humour: for instance, when the internal quarrelling of the characters gets out of hand, the Big Bad Wolf invariably calls them back to order, with a reminder of their duty towards the children who are, after all, watching the play. Tremblay also adds an unconventional twist to the traditional technique of audience involvement and direct actor-audience contact. He satirizes this convention by juxtaposing the usual polite form of address ("Oh, bonjour, les enfants!... quelle belle surprise... comment ça va") with vicious asides, which range from ordinary insults, such as "snotty-nosed brats," to a threat of downright violence in the case of the Wicked Fairy, who demands that "each one of these children should be killed and their members woven into a carpet."

Tremblay has deliberately integrated *Les Héros de mon enfance* with the mainstream of his dramatic opus through the character of the wicked fairy Carabosse, who looks and behaves like the character of Pierrette in *Les Belles-Soeurs*. Like Pierrette, the great Carabosse has also loved a "Johnny." Carabosse, too, was subsequently deserted when the object of her affections, "handsome as a god in his leather outfit," headed back to his native country, "the land of the hot dog," which attracts him more than her old-fashioned magic. Thus, under the appearance of a bit of light fluff, self-propelled by wit and charm, this musical, too, carries a serious "moral" and "political" message.

CHAPTER SIX

Towards Freedom and Ecstasy: Sainte Carmen

With *Sainte Carmen de la Main*, Tremblay's mystical tendencies, always present but often hidden beneath surface realism, finally come to the fore. *Sainte Carmen de la Main* and *Damnée Manon, Sacrée Sandra,* the two plays that conclude this phase of his dramatic opus, clearly represent a progression towards a more spiritual view of the universe and of human life. There is no break or sudden change, of course, but simply a shift of emphasis. After all, even the Duchesse de Langeais, that pathetic bundle of perverse sensuality, harboured an impossible dream of purity and asceticism. The novel element in Carmen is simply the fact that she is able to make her particular dream come true; in the process she achieves the full status of tragic heroine, saint and martyr.

Sainte Carmen de la Main represents Tremblay's most ambitious dramatic work to date, in form as well as underlying ideas. Its composition is based on a combination of elements from the two most "elevated" genres of western literature, opera and Greek tragedy. The structure follows the Greek pattern of alternation between episodes and chorus; the speeches are designed like operatic "scores." The setting of the work remains, however, that of a cheap cabaret on the Main; the language used throughout is the lowly *joual*, and the basic story line is anything but noble. Nevertheless, Tremblay achieves a perfect synthesis of the many disparate formal elements, and the work thus appears totally unified.

On the level of ideas, the underlying parable is presented in a way that conveys a range of meanings greater than that of any of the previous plays. Here again, we have a remarkable synthesis of apparent contradictions. There is a sordid element in the story of the murder of Carmen, yodelling queen of the Main, at the hands of an ordinary punk like Toothpick, who bears her a grudge because she once made fun of his undersized male organ. Yet, Carmen rises to genuinely tragic-heroic proportions in her defiance of the Establishment, represented by Maurice, owner of the cabaret. Carmen has decided to change her performance material from Western music, meaningless but remunerative, to songs she has written herself, in which she speaks to her listeners of their own lives and their own problems and tries to rouse them out of their lethargic acceptance of the status quo. When Maurice expressly forbids her to continue, Carmen refuses to give in and is promptly put to death by his henchman, Toothpick, who is only too glad of this opportunity for revenge. Carmen's death thus becomes true martyrdom; and her pulp press story becomes a parable of the individual's need to stand up to the Establishment, of the artist's freedom and mission, of the archetypal Saviour figure's inevitable destruction at the hands of an uncomprehending society. The image of Carmen as a Saviour figure is particularly emphasized through a number of liturgical details in the play, to which we will return later. The Saviour image also has political connotations in reference to Quebec society.

In *A toi, pour toujours, ta Marie-Lou*, the character Carmen represented the author's hopes for the future of his country. She was the first of his major female characters to achieve freedom from the triple tradition of moral discipline and bondage: family, the martyr complex and sexual taboos. But Tremblay's hopes for Quebec failed to materialize. The political situation in Quebec did not bear out the promise of the sixties, and as it became increasingly clear that there would be little change after the Quiet Revolution, Tremblay became more and more disenchanted. He now saw a parallel between the actions of his Carmen and the general trend of *québécois* society which, like

Carmen, had made a revolutionary break with the past, started on a radically new path and then, in the early seventies, seemed to have stopped dead in its tracks. Taking a second more critical and objective look at *A toi, pour toujours, ta Marie-Lou*, Tremblay concluded that although Carmen's original intention may have been right, her escape from the family to the Rodeo café provided no real solution to the overall problem of liberation: "Où c'est qu'a s'en va n'est guère plus beau que d'où elle vient..." [1] ("Where she is going is hardly better than where she's coming from..."). Less than a year after making this statement, Tremblay had finished his new Carmen play, *Sainte Carmen de la Main;* and this time, where she is going—to a tragic death in the pursuit of an ideal—is definitely "plus beau" than where she is coming from.

The second Carmen play, then, must be seen as a logical progression from the first, with Carmen now ready to go on, as Tremblay would put it, to the end of her "trip." Her final elevation to "sainthood" follows the pattern of existentialist ethics as developed by Sartre: from awareness to freedom, from freedom to responsibility, from responsibility to action. Action in this context necessarily brings about confrontation with the forces of the Establishment, and thus sets the stage for a tragic conclusion.

While "Sainte" Carmen achieves the absolute with her death as a martyr, Carmen in *A toi, pour toujours, ta Marie-Lou* remains strictly within the finite context of emancipation from the oppression of family, martyr syndrome and sexual taboos. She develops a concomitant sense of responsibility, but again, it remains within the confines of her family situation. Her missionary zeal extends no farther than her sister Manon.

Nevertheless, the character of Carmen in the first play represents a very real breakthrough. Carmen fully realizes that the family poses the major menace to her happiness, and she works up the determination to break out from what she refers to as "c'te maudite trappe à rats" ("this goddamn rat trap"). The difference in her life is dramatic: "Pour moé, tout a changé.... En dix ans, chus devenue une autre femme" (38-39) ("For me, everything has changed... In ten years, I have become a different woman"). While she triumphantly asserts her newly gained freedom and happiness, her sister Manon continues the same life of quiet desperation she led when her parents were still living; for Manon, nothing has changed, "c'est comme un grand ruban gris en arrière de moé... tout pareil" (40) ("it's like a large grey ribbon behind me... the same all over"). Nevertheless, from the heights of her moral eminence, Manon condemns her sister's lifestyle, the undignified look of her cowgirl outfit, the connotation of whore attached to her job. But Carmen remains unimpressed by her sister's pious exercises: "Pour moé, être libre, c'est chanter des chansons de cowboy au Rodéo, pis après! C'est toujours mieux que de rester gommé dans son passé, un chapelet à la main..." (70) ("For me, to be free means to sing cowboy songs at the Rodeo, so what! It's always better than to remain stuck in your past, your beads in your hand...").

Carmen's liberated, joyous lifestyle thus stands in direct antithesis to the traditional self-pitying martyr complex typical of so many females in French-Canadian literature. Manon provides a perfect example of this life-denying attitude which causes Carmen's despair. In an exasperated attempt to open her sister's eyes, Carmen reminds her of the time when Manon, just a small child, was asked what she wanted to be when she grew up and replied without the slightest hesitation, "Quand j'vas être grande, j'veux être ben, ben malheureuse, pis mourir martyre" (65) ("When I'm big, I want to be very, very unhappy, and then die as a martyr"). The pattern is exactly the pattern of her mother's life before her, and so on through the generations. It is ironic that Carmen, who absolutely refuses to accept the traditional role of the long-suffering victim and martyr, eventually achieves genuine martyrdom in the pursuit of freedom from this very tradition.

Finally, Carmen's liberation comes through a break with the sexual taboos that have kept generations of women before her in all the various stages of frustration, alienation and emotional aridity that we have met in Les Belles-Soeurs and other plays of the family cycle. Tremblay underlines the sharp contrast between the sexually liberated figure of Carmen and the archetypal Québécois women of the play: Marie-Louise, whose sex life through fifteen years of marriage reduces to four episodes of rape/impregnation, and Manon, the spinster who lives in (literally) holy terror of sex and finds her main emotional outlet in reciting her rosary. Carmen alone has achieved a normal, no-nonsense attitude. She responds with good-natured laughter to her sister's accusation that she is nothing but a whore, and freely admits that sex "isn't everything," but hastens to add, "ça aide à vivre quequ'chose de rare" (82) ("it sure helps you to live like nothing else on earth does"). Her relaxed attitude here contrasts sharply with Manon's tense and inhibited outlook.

Having achieved a measure of freedom, Carmen develops a sense of responsibility that is totally lacking in her morally upright, existentially uptight sister Manon. Carmen's tolerance and understanding give ironic emphasis to the self-centredness of her pious sister. While Manon feeds upon memories of her unhappy past and cultivates her feelings of hatred for her father, Carmen shows great compassion for the man, and tries to understand the enormous difficulties he must have gone through: "Y était pas plus écoeurant qu'un autre, Manon... Y était peut-être juste un peu plus écoeuré" (50) ("He wasn't any more disgusting than the next man, Manon... He was perhaps a bit more disgusted, that's all"). Here she already shows some of the traits that make her into the "Sainte" Carmen of the next play: understanding of her fellow men, tolerance for their weaknesses and, in the case of her sister Manon, an almost missionary zeal to help her extricate herself from the unhappy life in which she seems imprisoned. After all, the sole purpose of Carmen's visit to her inhospitable sister has been to make a final effort at prying her loose from her obsession with the past:

J'veux juste que tu sortes d'icitte... que tu sortes de tes rêves, un peu.... Y faudrait que tu comprennes qu'y'est temps que tu sacres ton chapelet à terre, que tu te débarrasses de tes saintes vierges en plâtre, que tu mettes la clef dans'porte, pis que tu te vides la tête de toute ça! Révolte-toé, Manon, c'est tout ce qui te reste! (45, 92) (I just want you to get out of here... to get out of your dream world for a bit.... You ought to understand that it's time for you to throw out your rosary, to get rid of all your holy virgins made out of plaster, to put the key in the lock, and to get all that stuff out of your head! Revolt, Manon, it's all you've got left!)

In *Sainte Carmen de la Main*, Carmen's call for rebellion and a new life is directed beyond the individual and addresses an entire society—all the poor, the downtrodden, the humble of the Main, to whom she wishes to give new hope. The political, social, religious and universally human implications are obvious. Her death, like that of every other Saviour figure, appears inevitable from the start. With this play, the character of Carmen reaches genuinely tragic proportions as she meets her fate in the exercise of her freely chosen artistic mission. In contrast to the impotence leitmotif of earlier Tremblay characters ("chus pas capable"), Carmen triumphantly asserts her newly gained sense of power: "chus capable, astheur" ("now, I can"). She knows exactly what she wants, she is capable of carrying it out, and she will defy anyone who stands in her way. For the first time in the Tremblay opus, we are presented with a central figure who is not an antihero, but a "heroic" character in the traditional sense of that word. Carmen, whose central image in the play is the sun, achieves a classical grandeur in spite of the sordid and anything but noble background of the story.

Conceived by Tremblay as an "opéra parlé" ("spoken opera"), *Sainte Carmen de la Main* is actually constructed along the lines of Greek tragedy. The play consists of the traditional overture designed to establish the theme (the *parodos*, or first choral song), a central portion alternating among solo parts, duos, trios and choral recitation (*episodes*), and a highly operatic "grand finale" (*exodos*). Actually, one cannot avoid the feeling that Tremblay is determined to parody ever so slightly the operatic genre, much as Brecht had done in his *Threepenny Opera*. These are, for example, the stage directions for Carmen's initial appearance during the first choral song: "Dans un bruit d'enfer, Carmen sort de l'ombre comme une apparition" (10) ("Amidst infernal noise, Carmen steps out of the darkness like an apparition"). In the same way, the excesses, both visual and auditory, of the finale appear to be somewhat tongue-in-cheek versions of the overpowering effects associated with grand opera. However, the speeches of the characters and, more important, of the two choruses are definitely composed and orchestrated along serious musical lines, with the same give-and-take of melodies and motifs that we have seen in the dialogues of *A toi, pour toujours, ta Marie-Lou*. The first lines of the play furnish a good example:

CHOEUR I: A matin, le soleil s'est levé

CHOEUR II: A matin

CHOEUR I: Le soleil

CHOEUR II: Je l'ai vu

CHOEURS I ET II: J'ai vu le soleil se lever, à matin, au bout d'la rue
Sainte-Catherine

(5)

In fact, the author has not only conceived the choral portions of *Sainte Carmen de la Main* as musical scores but he has also written them accordingly. On pages 116–17 is a portion of the "score" included in the printed version of the play.

Following the classical structure of Greek tragedy, *Sainte Carmen de la Main* consists of five episodes punctuated by choral passages and ending with the traditional epilogue. There is also a Christian element in the three gospel-like readings relating to the life of Carmen which her dresser, Bec-de-Lièvre (Harelip), recites at various strategic moments in the play. Although the settings, characters and language contrast sharply with the purity of the traditional form, Tremblay achieves remarkable poetic effects with his *joual* chorus, made up of the "transvestites of the Main," led by Sandra, and the "whores of the Main," led by Rose Beef.

The three essential elements in the poetry of the choral passages in *Sainte Carmen de la Main* are: traditional poetic devices (imagery, rhythm, sound effect); a structure that is based on a system of counterpoint and/or repetition; and the tone, which is largely determined by a contrast between ordinary language and the events described, with their extraordinarily poetic and universal significance.

Each of the two acts of *Sainte Carmen de la Main* is governed by a central image: the sun in act 1, symbol of the glory of Carmen; and thunder and lightning in act 2, foreshadowing her ultimate destruction. The opening chorus of the play, whose major function is to create the proper emotional climate for the eventual appearance of Carmen herself, revolves almost entirely around the sun image, which has multiple levels of evocative meaning, from radiance and beauty to stark vio-

A *À l'unisson, très lent*

CHOEUR I – 1 Le monde font la queue à porte du Rodéo.
CHOEUR II – Le monde font la queue à porte du Rodéo.
SANDRA –
ROSE BEEF – 2 Ça s'est pas vu depuis la fois que Carmen est partie.
CARMEN –
BEC-DE-LIÈVRE –

B

CHOEUR I – 22 24 Poussez pas! Poussez pas!
CHOEUR II – Poussez pas! Poussez pas!
SANDRA – 23 Aie, poussez pas!
ROSE BEEF – Poussez pas!
CARMEN –
BEC-DE-LIÈVRE – 25 Regardez, même Maurice est nerveux.

C

CHOEUR I – 38 (*Murmures.*) 39 (*Murmures de plus en plus prononcés.*)
CHOEUR II – (*Murmures.*) (*Murmures de plus en plus prononcés.*)
SANDRA – (*Murmures.*) (*Murmures de plus en plus prononcés.*)
ROSE BEEF – (*Murmures.*) (*Murmures de plus en plus prononcés.*)
CARMEN – On dirait qu'un orage se prépare! On pourrait couper l'électricité au couteau!
BEC-DE-LIÈVRE – On dirait qu'un orage se prépare! On pourrait couper l'électricité au couteau!

D

CHOEUR I – 51 Carmen! 53 À soir va être un grand soir! 54 À soir va être un grand soir!
CHOEUR II – Carmen! À soir va être un grand soir! À soir va être un grand soir!
SANDRA – Carmen! À soir va être un grand soir! À soir va être un grand soir!
ROSE BEEF – Carmen! À soir va être un grand soir! À soir va être un grand soir!
CARMEN – À soir va être un grand soir! À soir va être un grand soir!
BEC-DE-LIÈVRE – J'ai peur! 52 Ben voyons donc! J'y vas. Fais attention! Y'a pas de danger.

A

3   4   5   6

CHOEUR I —
CHOEUR II —
SANDRA — Les autres places sont | vides. | Maurice a même décidé de fermer le Coconut.
     vides.
ROSE BEEF —
CARMEN —
BEC-DE-LIÈVRE —   Détends-toé! Détends-toé!

B

26   27   28

CHOEUR I —
CHOEUR II —
SANDRA — Y regarde Tooth Pick d'une drôle de façon. | Tooth Pick est arrivé le premier! | Y'a pris la meilleure table!
     Tooth Pick est arrivé le premier!
ROSE BEEF —
CARMEN —
BEC-DE-LIÈVRE —

C

40   41   42

CHOEUR I —
CHOEUR II —
SANDRA —
ROSE BEEF — (*Rose Beef éclate de rire.*) | Le premier éclair!
CARMEN —
BEC-DE-LIÈVRE — J'sais pas pourquoi, mais j'ai peur, tout d'un coup, Carmen!

D

55   56 *Silence.*   57

CHOEUR I — À soir va être un grand soir! Carmen! Carmen!
CHOEUR II — À soir va être un grand soir! Carmen! Carmen!
SANDRA — À soir va être un grand soir! Carmen! Carmen!
ROSE BEEF — À soir va être un grand soir! Carmen! Carmen!
CARMEN — Chus sûre de c'que je fais! (*Carmen se dirige vers le fond.*)
BEC-DE-LIÈVRE —   À soir va être un grand soir!

lence. These opening lines constitute a carefully and effectively structured poem in their own right:

CHOEUR I: A matin, le soleil s'est levé

CHOEUR II: A matin

CHOEUR I: Le soleil

CHOEUR II: Je l'ai vu

CHOEURS I ET II: J'ai vu le soleil se lever, à matin, au bout d'la rue Sainte-Catherine

CHOEUR I: Une grosse boule de feu rouge

CHOEUR II: Sang

CHOEURS I ET II: Rouge sang

. . . .

Le soleil est venu au monde comme un coup de poing rouge au bout d'la Catherine!

SANDRA: C'tait beau!

ROSE BEEF: C'tait beau!

(5-6)

(CHORUS I: This morning, the sun arose

CHORUS II: This morning

CHORUS I: The sun

CHORUS II: I have seen it

CHORUSES I AND II: I have seen the sun rise, this morning, at the end of St. Catherine Street

CHORUS I: A large ball of fire, all red.

CHORUS II: Like blood

CHORUSES I AND II: Blood red

. . . .

The sun came to the world like a red fist at the end of the street!

SANDRA: It was beautiful!

ROSE BEEF: It was beautiful!)

The emotional ambiguity of the central image is expressed first in terms of a cycle—from beauty to violence and back to beauty—a mini-version of the emotional experience conveyed by the play as a whole. The author then enlarges the experience by adding a synesthetic perception ("On pourrait presque dire... que je l'ai entendu!" [7] ["You could almost say... I heard it!"]) and sexual overtones ("On arait dit que c'tait la première fois" [7] ["You would have thought it was the first time"]; "... à matin le soleil s'est levé pour la première fois sur la Catherine!" [9] ["... this morning the sun rose for the first time on St. Catherine Street!"]). Eventually, all the connotations come together in an overwhelming emotional experience: "Ah! Y'a explosé sans prévenir, pis chus restée clouée sur le coin de la Main avec... les larmes... aux yeux!" (9) ("Oh! It exploded without a warning, and there I was, unable to move, on the corner of the Main... tears in my eyes!"). This in turn leads to the final joyful ushering in of Carmen herself, who rises suddenly, sunlike, out of the shadows of the back of the stage.

The thrice-repeated thunder and lightning image in act 2 is less elaborate but equally rich in emotional overtones and associations: initially, the thunder indicates danger and a threat to Carmen's life, distant at first, then ever closer; next, it foreshadows the sound of Toothpick's gun as he commits the murder; and finally, the darkness closing in over the chorus in the last scene both suggests the end of hope and carries heavy overtones of the darkness at the moment of Christ's death on the Cross.

The structure of the play, too, merits close examination. It opens in the traditional manner, with the entry of the two choral groups and their respective leaders. They describe the morning's sunrise, heralding the return of Carmen, for "le soleil, c'est Carmen!" ("the sun, that's Carmen!"). Thus, the figure of Carmen is given symbolic significance from the very start, within an ultranaturalistic scene of bedraggled whores at the end of a night's work. Against this background of choral recitation, the figure of Carmen appears on stage, followed by Bec-de-Lièvre who proceeds in a ritual fashion to assist Carmen with her costume, "comme un enfant de choeur aide un prêtre à revêtir ses derniers ornements avant une cérémonie importante" (14) ("as a choirboy helps a priest to put on his final vestments before an important ceremony").

The first chorus, then, serves as introduction and exposition. The exposition continues into the first episode, where Carmen introduces herself to the audience through a long monologue addressed to Bec-de-Lièvre, who functions as the traditional confidante. Carmen is just back from an extended stay in the United States, where she has not only perfected her singing techniques but also discovered new powers within herself: "Chus capable, astheur! A soir, c'est mes propres paroles que j'vas chanter!" (14) ("I can do it now! Tonight, it's my own words I'm going to sing!"). Her monologue is interrupted by the brief appearance of Toothpick, who laconically announces his intention of "getting her": the plot is thus set. Left alone, Bec-de-Lièvre, the humble little lesbian who plays both acolyte and disciple to Carmen, recites to the audience the first of three gospel-like passages — all introduced by a ritual "y parait" ("they say that") — which throw light on certain aspects of Carmen's past and foreshadow the future. The first such reading tells of the birth of Carmen and of her mother Marie-Louise's unnatural and hostile attitude towards her first-born. The episode concludes on an ecstatic note, as Bec-de-Lièvre praises the charms of Carmen to the chorus leaders, and the three women reverently anticipate the evening's performance: "J'ai l'impression de me préparer à mourir d'amour" (19) ("I feel as if I were getting ready to die of love").

A brief recitation by the joint choruses separates episode 1 from episode 2. This chorus creates an atmosphere of expectation by cataloguing the activities of all the regulars of the Main as they get ready for the big night.

Episode 2 advances the action initiated by Toothpick's earlier appearance. It is mainly devoted to a confrontation that foreshadows the final and tragic conflict between Carmen and her boss/lover Maurice. Carmen demands that Maurice order the threatening Toothpick off the premises, but he refuses. However, Carmen insists that she will not perform with Toothpick around, and Maurice is finally forced to admit that Toothpick is a professional killer whose services he calls upon whenever he wants someone eliminated from his domain and whom he therefore cannot afford to antagonize. Carmen understands; but with a naiveté that appears ironic to the audience she still insists that Maurice should do "something." The episode creates a palpable sense of doom, which mounts as Carmen's old rival, Gloria, appears on the scene and threatens to destroy her.

The central portion of the play consists of two symmetrical choral scenes separated by a brief walk-on by Toothpick carrying a gun (episode 3). The first of these scenes (the third chorus of the play) picks up the sense of foreboding created by the preceding episode, as the chorus describes the strange atmosphere of hushed expectation in the crowded cabaret. Carmen feels the mounting tension and decides to begin her act, but then she spots Toothpick and Gloria in the room and recoils in terror. The voices of the chorus now become the voices of fate clamouring for Carmen to appear. Eventually, Maurice announces he will give the signal to start, and after a brief silence, which indicates that she is fully aware of what she is about to do, Carmen acquiesces and steps out onto the stage. Solemnly Bec-de-Lièvre intones a second gospel dealing with Carmen's first communion, which was marked by the same fear and eventual defiance as the present situation. This reading increases the anxiety of the moment by associating it with a frightening episode from the heroine's childhood.

Episode 3 uses an interesting device to emphasize the tragic sense of fatality: we never see Carmen's long-awaited performance, but instead we have a brief glimpse of Toothpick crossing the stage, gun in hand. Thus the author symbolically presages the heroine's fate, at the very moment of her greatest triumph.

In keeping with the conventions of classical tragedy, none of the action takes place on stage. Instead of witnessing Carmen's performance, the audience learns of her triumph indirectly from the chorus in the next scene. This device is extremely effective since no actual performance could possibly produce an effect to equal the chorus's delirious reaction. There is a complete reversal of tone here, from doom to ecstasy, as the members of the chorus come on stage reeling with joy. To the crowd of the Main, long since resigned to accepting their suffering and humiliation as an inevitable part of life, Carmen's song has brought an awakening:

CHOEUR I: Réveille-toé! (Wake up!)
CHOEUR II: Réveille-toé!
CHOEUR I: Lève-toé! (Get up!)
CHOEUR II: Lève-toé!
CHOEURS I ET II: Réveille-toé! Lève-toé! Lève-toé! Lève-toé!
(50)

The message carries very obvious social and political overtones, as well as a plea for individual liberation. Carmen has asked her audience to "wake up," but she has also tried to arouse in them a sense of self-worth, to make them see the importance of their own lives. Their grateful reaction is like that of a lost people exalting the prophet who points the way to salvation. For the first time, these poor, downtrodden, despised beings feel that someone has acknowledged their existence: "Carmen a parlé de moé!" ("Carmen has spoken about me!"). Someone has seen beauty in the life of every whore, transvestite or lesbian: "Pis a l'a dit que c'était pas laid!" ("And she said it isn't ugly!"). Most important, she has given them hope: "Pis Carmen a chanté que j'pourrais ben me réveiller un jour" ("In her song, Carmen also said I might well wake up, one of these days"). The last line, repeated many times over, carries with it not only an element of hope but also a political threat, for "Carmen a dit qu'au fond de moé—j'étais forte!" ("Carmen said that deep down, I am strong!"). In the final lines of this chorus, Carmen takes on the character of a Christ figure, a prophet who brings a message of salvation to the down-and-out:

BEC-DE-LIEVRE: Tout le monde m'a toujours dit que j'étais laide!
SANDRA: Que j'étais vulgaire!
ROSE BEEF: Que j'savais pas parler!
CHOEURS I ET II: Que j'étais sale!
TOUS: Tout le monde a toujours eu honte de moé! Mais Carmen

m'a dit que j'étais belle pis que j'pourrais sortir de la taverne! (*Silence*) Sortir de la taverne!

CHOEUR I: Réveille-toé, qu'a l'a dit!

CHOEUR II: Lève-toé, qu'a l'a dit!

SANDRA, ROSE BEEF, BEC-DE-LIEVRE: Reste pas effouerrée de même!

TOUS: Reste pas assis! Reste pas assis! J'vas t'aider! (*Silence*) Carmen m'a offert de m'aider. Ah! J'oublierai jamais sa dernière chanson!

(52–53)

(BEC-DE-LIEVRE: Everyone has always told me I'm ugly!

SANDRA: That I am vulgar!

ROSE BEEF: That I don't know how to talk!

CHORUSES I AND II: That I am dirty!

ALL: Everybody has always been ashamed of me! But Carmen said I am beautiful and that I might be able to get out from the tavern! [*Silence*] Get out from the tavern!

CHORUS I: Wake up, she said!

CHORUS II: Get up, she said!

SANDRA, ROSE BEEF, BEC-DE-LIEVRE: Don't stay put like that!

ALL: Don't just sit there! Don't just sit there! I'll help you! [*Silence*] Carmen has offered to help me. Oh! I won't ever forget her last song!)

Toothpick's appearance is thus very effectively framed by two choral scenes which balance each other emotionally: one spells doom and the other, hope. But the joyful tone of the last chorus takes on an ironic overtone as the plot moves towards its tragic conclusion. The next episode (episode 4) shows the final conflict between Maurice and Carmen. This scene parallels their earlier confrontation, but this time we witness a clash of ideologies rather than a conflict over practical matters. The scene is strongly reminiscent of the confrontation between Creon and Antigone, as Maurice defends his commonsense standpoint against a Carmen determined to pursue her ideal regardless of consequences. Carmen grows in stature in response to Maurice's opposition. At first she is almost certain that he can be convinced, but she gradually realizes that their differences are irreconcilable and that she must defy him if she wishes to preserve her personal and artistic integrity.

When Maurice bursts into Carmen's dressing room and forbids her ever to repeat her performance, she refuses outright. Her response is a long monologue in which she tries to explain to Maurice her new-found insights about the importance of her role as an artist and the responsibility she feels towards her audience. Beyond the universal significance of her defence of artistic freedom, her speech strongly suggests Quebec's need and desperate search for a truly national cultural identity, not one imposed, like Western folklore, from the outside. She points out the futility of talking about cowboys riding into the sunset to her own people, the people who live around the Main: "Y'a jamais personne qui leur a parlé d'eux-autres!... as-tu entendu c'que ça leur fait quand ma voix leur parle directement à eux-autres dans leurs mots à eux-autres... la Main a besoin qu'on y parle de la Main!" (59) ("Nobody has ever talked to them about themselves!... did you hear what it does to them when my voice speaks to them directly, in their own words... the Main needs to hear about the Main!"). The last phrase could well serve as a rationale for all the *joual* dramas of Michel Tremblay!

Carmen's idealism fails to convince the cynical Maurice. Not only is he afraid that the girl's zeal to help her people may in the long run empty his establishment but he is also convinced that her attempt is futile. The argument here goes well beyond the political sphere to take on universal and religious overtones, as Maurice tries to convince Carmen that those for whom she is ready to give her life do not even wish to be saved. This, of course, is the standard argument of one in power who wants to avoid any change in a status quo that suits him well.

Carmen refuses to accept such a defeatist attitude, however. Her success has filled her with new confidence in those whom Maurice despises. She is sure that they are indeed capable of salvation, if only given half a chance, and so she pleads with Maurice to at least let her try. He responds to her entreaties with a sneer, and she is forced into defiance and a clear statement of her position: "La Main mérite de vivre mais il faut l'aider à s'en rendre compte! J'ai commencé à soir,

Maurice, pis j'arrêterai certainement pas là! J'me sens assez sure de moé pis assez forte pour te tenir tête..." (64) ("The Main deserves to live, but you have to help make them aware of it! I've started tonight, Maurice, and I'm certainly not going to stop there! I feel sure enough of myself and strong enough to stand up to you..."). Like Antigone defying Creon, Carmen seals her own fate with this uncompromising affirmation of her principles. Maurice leaves, and she is filled with a sense of exaltation as she realizes that for her there is no turning back. From now on she must follow the unswerving path that the tragic hero travels towards his doom. For the moment, Carmen is aware only of the serenity that comes from profound conviction: "Chus contente, parce que j'peux pus reculer. Q'y arrive n'importe quoi, j'vas être obligée de continuer, d'aller plus loin, astheur. C'est-tu assez merveilleux, y a pas de r'venez-y!" (65) ("I'm glad, because I can't go back any longer. Whatever happens, I'll have to continue, to go further from now on. Isn't it fabulous, there's no more turning back!"). Thus, the fourth episode ends on a note of personal triumph for Carmen. It also makes a tragic ending unavoidable.

The final choral interlude provides a background for the murder of Carmen. Following the classical convention, the act of violence itself will later take place off-stage; there is a great deal of dramatic irony in the fact that the chorus is on stage announcing its concern to the audience as the victim is being killed (the technique parallels exactly that of Aeschylus in the scene depicting the murder of Agamemnon).

As the chorus re-enters it is still under the spell of Carmen's performance. The joy and sense of purification that the people of the Main now feel bear out Carmen's belief in their ultimate potential for redemption: "On dirait que quelqu'un... est après me laver à grande eau..." (67) ("I feel as if someone had given me a good bath..."). Then Rose Beef casually mentions the name of Toothpick, and the atmosphere gradually changes. Carmen's offhand reaction becomes a source of dramatic irony. She is sure of herself now, and even the faithful Bec-de-Lièvre seems to relax ("he's not important"), but the sound of a gunshot, "like distant thunder," recalls the lightning storm image and Carmen's earlier panic; this is the signal for an increasing buildup of tension and anxiety. Another shot rings out, and the chorus now surrounds Carmen protectively, trying to keep her away from the shower room at the other end of the corridor. The chorus reinforces its argument by repeating the same refrain, "Prends pas ta douche, Carmen, vas pas là!" ("Don't take a shower, Carmen, don't go there!"), and variations on that theme ("there is no more soap"; "there are no towels"; "there is no more hot water"). Carmen, however, is unconcerned. Dramatic irony reaches a new peak as the joint choruses thrice repeat the highly ambiguous line, "Tout le monde va fêter. c'te nuitte" ("Tonight everyone celebrates"), just as Carmen makes her exit towards the fateful shower and death. It is at this point that Bec-de-Lièvre gives her third, and last, gospel reading, on the joint themes of death and salvation. She tells how Carmen's parents, Léopold and Marie-Louise, died in a car accident and how Carmen reacted to their death as a deliverance. As Bec-de-Lièvre follows Carmen off-stage, the chorus comments on the sudden darkness outside, which is punctuated by lightning, and the scene evokes Christ's death on the Cross. Then, from off-stage, comes Bec-de-Lièvre's scream of horror, which only confirms what the audience already knows has happened.

In the final scene of classical tragedy a narrator comes on and tells of the catastrophe, but in *Sainte Carmen de la Main* this traditional device gains a special ironic twist when the murderer himself arrives to tell the tale. Maurice has mentioned in an earlier scene that Toothpick is a man of great imagination. This is now borne out by the killer's long and involved story, which credits Bec-de-Lièvre with killing Carmen in a fit of lesbian jealousy. The chorus does not protest; the only sound is a soft-spoken, ambiguous "ah!"—followed by silence. The grand finale is anticlimactic: in an apotheosis of vulgarity, Gloria appears and takes over Carmen's place. This ending, which stresses the futility of Carmen's sacrifice, sets *Sainte Carmen de la Main* apart from classical tragedy; in keeping with his generally pessimistic and cynical outlook, the author has chosen to abort any possible catharsis.

Sainte Carmen de la Main has met with more negative reaction from both critics and audiences than any of Michel

Tremblay's plays since *Les Belles-Soeurs*. The play premiered in the summer of 1976 as part of the cultural festival connected with the Montreal Olympics, but folded after only three performances. Later that year, the Jean Duceppe company, which had planned to open its fall season with *Sainte Carmen de la Main*, also took it off the program for fear of incurring a large deficit. In June 1978, the play was at least partly rehabilitated in a new production by the Théâtre du Nouveau Monde.

It is not difficult to imagine why *Sainte Carmen de la Main* failed to appeal to a large public; it is, however, hard to understand why the critics failed to appreciate it. The play was a shock to the audience, which had come to expect a surface realism from Tremblay. This play is unlike all his previous dramas, whose main interest is in the characters. *Sainte Carmen de la Main* is also highly theatrical, a factor that inhibits immediate identification. The chief merits of this work, definitely the most complex in the author's opus to date, lie in its intricate composition, itself an aesthetic tour de force; in Tremblay's ability to make the ordinary *joual* into a vehicle of utmost poetic impact; and in the multiple levels of interpretation suggested by the incidents and imagery of the plot. Nevertheless, characterization is also a strong point. This is especially true of Carmen, who always maintains exactly the right balance between the no-nonsense attitudes of a working-class woman and the exaltation of a prophet and missionary. Because she expresses herself in the language of the people, she does not seem at odds with the other characters from the Main.

Critics of the play were irritated primarily by the fact that Tremblay had adopted a classical genre, which they felt was outmoded and inappropriate for a modern audience accustomed to less demanding forms. Other critics were indignant at the implication that the riffraff of the Main might be a valid symbol of the people of Quebec. This, at least, was an understandable response (echoes of *Les Belles-Soeurs*!). Less understandable were a number of reviews, including one by Micheline Cambron in the academically respectable *Livres et auteurs québécois*,[2] which argued that the audience is cheated out of the central experience of the play, Carmen's inspirational song. It seems fairly obvious that Tremblay is using the song as a symbol of the different dreams and aspirations of many people and that to try to make such a symbol into something real would destroy the very idea and render it absurd.

Tremblay himself commented on this issue in the program notes for the 1978 production of *Sainte Carmen de la Main*. Under the heading "A chacun son Godot" ("To Each His Own Godot"), he explained that if he did not write Carmen's songs into the play, it was not because he knows little about Western music, but rather because it never occurred to him:

Ces chansons sont beaucoup moins importantes que leur impact sur le choeur. Le choeur a trouvé dans les cris d'amour de Carmen des choses que je n'aurais peut-être pas su y mettre... il est beaucoup plus intéressant pour chaque spectateur de s'imaginer les chansons de Carmen.... Ecoutez le choeur... soyez témoin de cette joie incontrôlable, de cette découverte de soi, de ce réveil.... Pour ma part, j'attends toujours Godot et pourtant je sais que s'il arrivait... ce serait une des plus grandes déceptions de ma vie. A chacun son Godot.[3] (The songs are much less important than their impact on the chorus. The chorus has found in Carmen's outcries of love things that I perhaps would not have been able to put there... it is much more interesting for the spectator to imagine the songs of Carmen. ... Listen to the chorus... witness this uncontrollable joy, this self-discovery, this awakening.... As for me, I am still waiting for Godot, and yet I know that if he were to show himself... it would be one of the greatest disappointments of my life. To each his own Godot.)

Although the original production of *Sainte Carmen de la Main* followed the stylized conventions of Greek tragedy, with an all-white setting and Carmen dressed in white, André Brassard staged his 1978 production in the modern style. The chorus now appeared as "genuine" down-and-outs from the big city, and the setting, a background of flashing neon lights and broken-down façades that evoked exactly the spirit of the Main, was characterized by a minute naturalism which would have done credit to Stanislavsky. In this colourful but extraordinarily sordid setting, Carmen appeared as a very obvious sun symbol, dressed in a bikini-type cowgirl outfit of flashing gold lamé; her costume was calculated to appeal to an audience hungry for bold effects. This style of production appears to be more in line with the tastes of theatre audiences; however, in the text itself the serious reader will discover the aesthetic and intellectual qualities of *Sainte Carmen de la Main*.

CHAPTER SEVEN

The Sacred and the Profane: Damnée Manon, Sacrée Sandra

How to dominate reality?
Love is one way, imagination another.

Irving Layton

As we have seen earlier, the dramatic universe of Michel Tremblay consists of three self-contained spheres, each with its own set of characters: the rue Fabre, the Main, the Great Beyond. In the last play of the cycle, *Damnée Manon, Sacrée Sandra*, the three spheres finally merge into one — as logically they must, since this work is set within the mind of the poet himself, with the protagonists Manon and Sandra representing opposite and complementary aspects of their creator's personality. Seen in this light, the play stands out as the most autobiographical of Tremblay's works, an intimate confession whose relevance goes far beyond that of the purely personal details provided by the glimpses of characters and situations in *Bonjour, là, bonjour* or *En pièces détachées*.

Although the real locus of the play is psychological, Tremblay has also provided a solidly realistic physical setting. The fusion of the three worlds in the poet's mind is parallelled by a similar fusion on the physical level: Manon, daughter of Marie-Louise and Léopold, sister of Carmen, belongs to the world of the rue Fabre; Sandra the transvestite represents the world of the Main; both of them aspire to transcendence into a

Great Beyond through the exercise of their particular mysticism—religious for Manon, sexual for Sandra. The setting of the play is the rue Fabre and here the three worlds come together materially, as well. Manon, of course, has lived on the rue Fabre all her life. Sandra, born "on the same day and in the same house" as Manon, has eventually returned and taken a room near Manon's. As the play progresses the two characters engage in separate but obviously parallel monologues, as they pursue their individual obsessions across the street from each other: Manon, the spinster, seeks religious ecstasy through mystical union; Sandra, the transvestite, seeks sexual ecstasy through homosexual union. The two characters are well aware of each other's presence, and eventually discover—or better, reveal—that they are one. The leitmotif of the play thus becomes apparent: sensuality and religious fanaticism must be seen as two aspects of the basically same pursuit of the absolute that haunts all men and women. As the author himself put it, rather unceremoniously, "la religion et le sexe, c'est tout le même kit" [1] ("religion and sex, it all comes to the same, really"). The flippancy of the remark should not deceive us. Tremblay's deep concern with ways and means of breaking out of the limitations of a finite and rational world reveals a profoundly troubled spirit, obviously still haunted by the religion of his childhood and, like Nietzsche, raging at God for His failure to exist. [2]

Damnée Manon, Sacrée Sandra gives expression, for the first time, to a trend that runs through French-Canadian literature from the beginning, the tension between surface puritanism and a repressed sensuality: Gilles Marcotte, for instance, speaks of "une hantise bien québécois de la chair" [3] ("a typically Québécois sense of being haunted by the flesh"). Jacques Languirand comes close to the same idea, when he describes the basic theme of French-Canadian literature as a conflict between the Apollonian and the Dionysian elements, which reflects a society of repressed Dionysians forced to live like Apollonians. [4]

This tension, which is typical of all Puritanical societies, has its roots in the historical evolution of French Canada, which favoured the development of a strong power structure by the religious authorities. The founding years of Nouvelle France fall into the highly evangelical period of the Jansenist counterrevolution. The morality that developed among French Canadians thus closely parallelled the Puritanism of English-speaking settlers. The Catholic Church represented a powerful force from the beginning; the arrival of new orders, especially the Jesuits (1611), laid the foundation for what would become a virtual theocracy. Following the Conquest, the Church not only assumed an even stronger leadership but also became the rallying point for a growing nationalism, as the French language and the Catholic religion became linked in one and the same patriotic cause. The Church, then, must be seen as the dominant cultural as well as moral and spiritual influence. The Church in French Canada chose to follow unflinchingly the path laid out by the early Church fathers in their total con-demnation of a life lived according to the physical passions. The same Church that encouraged the Revenge of the Cradle pronounced sex anathema and blissfully ignored the paradoxi-cal, nay quixotic aspect of its position. The result of this long historical development appears, in retrospect, perfectly logical: contemporary literature, reflecting contemporary society, shows an absence of both sexual and spiritual health, pro-longed tension between the two poles having apparently done away with both! Pierre Vallières uses the example of his own parents to describe the loss of the capacity to love: "mes parents ne connurent jamais l'amour, mais firent semblant de s'aimer, comme des milliers de Québécois ont fait et font encore" [5] ("my parents never knew love, but pretended to love each other, as thousands of Québécois have done and still do"). The literary/dramatic equivalent is expressed very clearly in the couples of Marcel Dubé's plays, *mal-aimés* from first to last.

Michel Tremblay attacks, then, the problem of the two great "absences" of modern life, especially of modern life in Quebec: the absence of true spirituality and the absence of healthy sexuality. Each of the two modes of being is seen as a possible path in the pursuit of happiness: "Dans *Damnée Manon, Sacrée Sandra*, j'ai voulu prouver que la religion et le sexe pro-viennent d'un même besoin d'absolu. . . . On a fini par inventer Dieu parce qu'on en avait besoin. La même chose pour le sexe qui, lui, a été inventé à quatre-vingt-quinze pour cent" [6] ("In

Damnée Manon, Sacrée Sandra, I wanted to prove that religion and sex come from one and the same desire for an absolute. . . . Men ended up inventing God because they needed him. The same applies to sex, ninety-five per cent of which was invented as well"). Marie-Claire Blais has taken up a similar theme in two of her novels. In *Le Loup,* we find a juxtaposition of characters very similar to the tandem Manon-Sandra: Pierre, the idealistic medical student, and Bernard, the sensualist, both of whose pursuits eventually come to the same end. The equation of religious ecstasy and sexual ecstasy is developed in detail through the character of Héloise in *Une Saison dans la vie d'Emmanuel,* a girl who goes from the ascetic excesses of the convent to the sensual excesses of the brothel without becoming aware of a difference between the two. The work of Blais and Tremblay on this theme eloquently attests to modern post-Freudian man's loss of innocence. The strongly erotic element of most traditional mystical literature is now clear, but at the time of writing, the mystics (Catherine of Siena, Theresa of Avila, St. John of the Cross) must have been no more than dimly aware of the ambiguous nature of the emotions described.

Tremblay certainly cannot be accused of any such naiveté. A detailed analysis of *Damnée Manon, Sacrée Sandra* will show that the structure of the play involves explicit parallels and juxtapositions which indicate the complementary nature of the two characters and the consequent equation of religious and sexual mysticism.

This equation becomes most obvious through the author's use of parallel or complementary imagery. From the moment the lights go up, the audience is faced with a stage image clearly suggestive of two halves of one whole: on one side, Sandra, all dressed in white in a room painted black; on the other, Manon, all dressed in black, in a room painted white. Their very first speeches set the characters and underline their parallel aspirations:

MANON: La solution à toute . . . c'est le bon Dieu.

SANDRA: Y'a pas de qui, y'a pas de quand, de où, de pourquoi, la réponse, c'est toujours le cul.

(27)

(MANON: The solution for everything . . . is the good Lord.

SANDRA: There's no question of who, or when, where or why, the answer is always ass.)

They both come to the same conclusion as they meditate on their particular obsession, so that the next lines are spoken by both simultaneously: "Des fois j'me demande à quoi j'pouvais ben penser avant de penser à ça! (*Silence*) J'm'en rappelle pus! J'tais trop petite!" (30) ("Sometimes I wonder what I could have been thinking of before I thought of that! [*Silence*] I can't remember! I was too little!").

This brief passage, which serves as an introduction, is followed by the main portion of the play, identified by the author as the "confessions." In their confessions, each character takes us through the activities of the day, which follow a pattern consisting of complementary variations on basically identical situations: Manon awakens in the morning, Sandra in the afternoon; both have a sudden, inexplicable impulse to purchase a particularly outrageous tool to be used in the exercise of their separate professions or avocations — a grotesquely oversized rosary in the case of Manon, a grotesquely coloured set of lipstick and nail polish for Sandra. From here on, the dialectic pattern evolves around three major juxtapositions: (1) The red rosary versus the green lipstick. (2) The erotic use of a religious object (the rosary) versus the religious use of an erotic object (the lipstick). (3) The saint as sinner (Manon's nightmare about her statue of the Virgin) versus the sinner as saint (the statue of the Virgin used as a model for transvestite disguise). Each of these deserves closer analysis.

1. *The red rosary versus the green lipstick.* Tremblay's device of using complementary colours for the two objects instantly calls the attention of the audience or reader to their parallel function as physical props in the characters' pursuit of ecstasy, whether it be religious or sexual. Manon relates the story of her purchase first. She has gone all the way to the Oratoire St. Joseph, Montreal's famous pilgrim shrine, to look for a larger and especially heavy rosary, since she feels she can no longer pray effectively with the ordinary "cheap" little beads she has at

home. When she spots an unusually big and beautiful speci-men she reacts to it as if she has fallen in love: "Quand je l'ai vu celui-là, ça m'a donné comme un choc" (31) ("When I looked at that one, it gave me a real shock"). She knows this is the rosary she must have, even though it is obviously designed for institutional rather than private use, and is much too expensive for her limited budget. As she admires the magnificence of the beads, which are a beautiful colour, "red like wine," and the large black crucifix, her excitement knows no bounds. She asks to touch the rosary and feels it come alive in her hands, heavy and warm: "J'avais les larmes aux yeux. Pis j'avais d'la misère à parler..." (33) ("My eyes were full of tears. I could hardly talk..."). Eventually, she manages to tell the saleslady that she "needs" it (the term is significant!) right away, and happily returns home with her treasure safely packed in a large shop-ping bag.

In contrast to Manon's serious and sincere tone, Sandra's speech is flippant, cynical and full of a bawdy sort of humour. She describes in detail her activities upon awakening, which in-clude a half-amused, half-bored inspection of her physical assets and a bit of inconsequential masturbation. Eventually she gives in to a sudden impulse to acquire the kind of green lipstick and nail polish she remembers from the time when she was still a boy, known in the neighbourhood as little Michel. The outrageous colour had been worn by Michel's cousin Hélène, a beautiful but somewhat eccentric woman, con-demned by her more conservative neighbours. Almost hoping that the items in question are no longer available, Sandra makes her way to the corner drugstore, and is immediately handed what she asks for. And so she brings her purchase home, wondering what her lover's reaction to her find will be.

2. *The erotic use of a religious object versus the religious use of an erotic object.* On returning home with her new rosary, Manon can hardly wait to try it out. However, she feels she must not use it to pray, since it has not yet been blessed. She cannot resist the temptation to go over it tentatively, though, carefully touching each bead with her fingers. When she comes to the crucifix, she has a moment's hesitation, but finally gives in to her overpowering desire—with electrifying results:

J'ai passé longtemps les mains sur le corps de Notre-Seigneur qui a
tant souffert pour nous-autres... pis tout d'un coup... J'ai senti
comme un besoin... j'ai senti un besoin effrayant de
l'embrasser... J'comprenais pas... J'avais la croix dans les mains,
pis... Tout d'un coup j'me suis mis à embrasser le corps de Notre-
Seigneur comme si ça avait été la dernière affaire que je ferais dans
ma vie! J'tais sûre que j'étais pour mourir... foudroyée, après! La
joie! La joie pure! J'avais comme des bulles de bonheur qui
m'éclataient dans le coeur.... (43-44) (For a long time, I ran my
hands over the body of our Lord who has suffered so much for
us... then suddenly... I felt like a need... I felt a terrifying need to
kiss him... I didn't understand... I held the crucifix in my hands,
then... Suddenly I started to kiss the body of our Lord as though it
was the last thing I would do in my life! I was sure I was going to
die... struck by lightning afterwards! The joy! The pure joy of it! It
was like bubbles of happiness bursting in my heart....)

When it is all over, she puts the rosary into the hands of the life-
sized statue of the Virgin Mary which she keeps in her room
and happily settles down to sleep, smiling conspiratorily at His
mother.

Meanwhile, back in her room, Sandra also plays with her
new acquisitions, fantasizing about the possible uses she could
put them to when her lover Christian, a handsome young black
from Martinique, returns from work in the evening. Starting
with an innocently erotic idea ("it's sure to be his first green
blow job"), she slowly slips from erotic to religious fantasy as
she dreams of writing her own version of the "Bible" onto her
lover's back, in green lipstick: "J'vas écrire un livre porno-
graphique sur son corps. Ma Bible à moé. La Genèse selon
Sandra... Le Pentateuque, le Cantique des cantiques,
l'Ancien Testament pis le Nouveau Testament selon Sandra-la-
Verte! Pis surtout, l'Apocalypse selon moé!" (45-46) ("I'm
going to write a pornographic book on his body. My own Bible.
Genesis according to Sandra... The Pentateuch, the Song of
Songs, the Old and the New Testament according to Green
Sandra! And above all, the Apocalypse according to me!").
Her fantasies border on the blasphemous as she imagines
Christian, his black body besmeared with green, glued to her
cream-coloured satin sheets in the attitude of Christ crucified,
and herself on her knees next to the bed, reverent in the

presence of the "first Black God." In contrast to Manon's, Sandra's speech ends on a note of cynicism and discontent.

3. *The saint as sinner versus the sinner as saint.* In spite of her earlier, pleasantly orgasmic experience with her rosary, Manon's sleep is troubled by a nightmare that leaves her deeply disturbed, as well as indignant, because the Lord has allowed something evil to happen to her while she was defenceless in her sleep. In her dream, Manon's statue of the Virgin Mary takes on the features of the beautiful but evil Hélène, Michel's cousin. Having come to Hélène's door one day to call on her friend Michel, Manon fled in terror when Hélène appeared, made up with green lipstick complemented by green nail polish. Screaming that she had seen the devil, Manon ran to her mother, who confirmed her fears, and together they prayed that this demon might be removed from their neighbourhood. In her dream, Manon now sees her beloved Virgin Mary smirking at her with green lips, while her hands, tipped by green fingernails, make obscene gestures with the precious rosary. Despite Manon's protests, the statue then begins to caress her gently, just as she herself had earlier caressed the body of the Lord on the crucifix. Manon cannot fight off the ecstatic effect: "Oui, c'était doux! pis c'était bon!" (51) ("Yes, it felt good! It was sweet!"). Eventually, Manon throws herself on God's mercy to help her overcome the agonies of guilt.

While Manon battles her nightmare, Sandra meditates on the choice of a costume for the evening. Having lost all traces of real identity during her long years as a transvestite whore, role playing has become her second and, by now, real nature. She takes great pride in surprising her lovers with ever new "compositions"—a variation on the repertoire of impersonations we have met in the case of the Duchesse de Langeais. Inspired by her previous fantasies, she hits upon a highly original idea: "the Virgin Mary herself will welcome a Black from Martinique in her bed tonight." The image takes on a decidedly blasphemous tone as Sandra visualizes the effect she will create:

J'vas rester deboute dans le coin de ma chambre, dans ma robe blanche, mon manteau bleu pis ma petite ceinture dorée...J'vas rester immobile. Les bras écartés. Le sourire figé. Mais vert!... Sainte Sandra la Verte...Je suis l'Immaculée Conception! Pis c'est à soir que le Moineau Noir de l'Esprit Saint va venir me visiter.... (55-56) (I will remain standing in the corner of my room, in my white dress, my blue coat and my little gold belt... I won't move. Arms at the side. A fixed smile. But green!... Holy Sandra, the green saint... I am the Immaculate Conception! And tonight the Black Sparrow of the Holy Ghost will come to visit me....)

This image and Manon's dream have turned saint and sinner into reverse reflections of each other, illusions of the ego distorted by a more powerful id. Freud's pair of essays entitled "Instincts and Their Vicissitudes" and "Repression" could suitably serve as headings for the confessions of Sandra and Manon, where black and white, red and green, virtue and vice are revealed as opposite but easily interchangeable poles.

Following the three sets of parallel "confessions" that make up the bulk of the work, both characters reveal more about themselves and their relationship to each other in monologues, which lead to the climactic reunion of the two at the end of the play. Let us take a closer look, then, at the way in which the dramatist achieves the effect of two opposite but complementary characters merging into one.

Like the two modes of being that the characters represent, their speech is also diametrically opposed in tone. Whereas Manon's monologues are serious and intense and use a vocabulary that reflects the religious context of her life, Sandra's tone is flippant, ironic and sometimes vulgar. Her vocabulary comes from the world of sexuality and sensuality. As one would expect, Sandra's monologues are more colourful and lively than those of Manon, and this difference helps to accentuate the polar opposites that the characters represent — transvestite whore versus religious prude. In keeping with her profession and lifestyle, Sandra does not shrink from the use of vulgar expressions, such as "chier" ("shit") or the occasional *sacre;* she also makes free use of all the terms connected with the sexual act in general and the homosexual act in particular. These terms are almost trademarks of her profession, but she also shows a remarkable linguistic imagination. Her monologues

are filled with highly picturesque expressions and clever metaphors, which give her speeches a sustained liveliness and vi-
brancy. Almost every page contains examples of her imagistic
wit. In her first long dialogue, for example, she is describing
her decision to buy the green cosmetics, and the restlessness
preceding it as she tosses around, sleepless, in bed: "Entéka,
j'ai essayé de me rendormir; pas moyen. Et que j'm'la retourne
d'un bord et que j'm'la retourne de l'autre, rien à faire...
J'avais le mal de mer ça fait que chus sorti de ma nacelle pis j'ai
sauté dans mes culottes" (39) ("In any case, I tried to go back to
sleep; nothing doing. And so I turn to one side and I turn to the
other, no good... I was getting seasick, so I disembarked from
my gondola and jumped into my trousers"). There is a picturesque and slightly ironic element in all of Sandra's descriptions;
for instance, she refers to her dingy apartment as "mon palais
des mille et une nuits humides" ("my palace of the thousand
and one damp nights") and to the corner pharmacist, a fellow
homosexual who used to be a religious, as "vieille carcasse de
frère décapotable" ("old carcass of a convertible brother"). This
constant flow of concrete imagery makes Sandra's speeches so
entertaining that the audience never feels the absence of
physical action.

Sandra also has a strong sense of humour, which is expressed in terms of clever and sometimes very risqué or even
downright blasphemous puns, as well as good-natured satire
and a cynical self-appraisal that is both ironic and resigned.
Irony also resides in Sandra's deliberate alternation between
joual and a somewhat baroque type of "elegant" French; the
humorous effect is heightened by the fact that both kinds of
language occur within the same sentence. For instance, Sandra
says of examining herself: "Mais je regardais surtout ma super-
duper quéquette queen size et si tant belle" ("But I especially
looked at my super-duper tail, queen size and beautiful to
behold"). The anglicisms, so typical of the *québécois* dialect, in
the first part of the sentence seem ridiculous in contrast to the
poetic-archaic quality of "si tant belle," and the overall effect is
irresistibly funny. In a slightly different vein, Sandra is talking
about her sudden impulse to buy the green lipstick and
carrying on in purest *joual*, when she suddenly switches to the

tone of the sophisticated woman of the world with a statement evoking the atmosphere of a Parisian boudoir: "C'tu fou. Du vert!... J'ai de la misère à supporter un rouge un tant soit peu foncé à cause de mon teint capricieux" (39) ("Crazy, ain't it! Green!... I have the greatest difficulty in tolerating even a slightly darker shade of red because of my delicate complexion"). The combination of these linguistic styles creates a character who is immensely entertaining and who engages our attention throughout.

Manon is appealing, too, because of the sincerity and naiveté of her religious aspirations ("the Virgin and I, we smiled at each other"), and the pathos of her desperate desire for mystical ecstasy. The audience is well aware of the sexual implications of innocent Manon's religious exercises, and this provides the added benefit of dramatic irony. Although a more serious character than Sandra, Manon is not entirely without humour. She herself mentions that she has the gift of making people laugh at her amusing comparisons. Of course, her type of humour is a far cry from Sandra's raunchiness. In keeping with her character, Manon's style of expression remains well within the confines of an imagination ruled by religious concepts.

As drawn by Tremblay, the two personalities are as thoroughly complementary as their actions. Sandra's character is based on an insatiable sensuality. She freely admits that her entire life has been dedicated to the pursuit of the pleasures of the flesh. As soon as she wakes up, she inspects herself from head to toe and comes away with a great sense of satisfaction: "Mes petites mains fines et souples... savantes, experimentées, vicieuses; mes mignons petits pieds, trottinant fermes et légers en amour;... mes bras, ah! mes bras: des ailes... que dis-je, des ailes, des plumes! Pas d'autruche, de cygne!" (36) ("My supple little hands... clever, experienced, vicious; my darling little feet, trotting towards love firmly and lightly;... my arms, ah! my arms: wings... what am I saying, wings, feathers! Not ostrich feathers, swan feathers!"). The perfection of her sexual parts sends her into raptures, and she concludes the exercise with a triple "bravo!" addressed to herself.

However, her triumph is short-lived, because even the pleasure she takes in her own physique and its potential for pleasure is not strong enough to counterbalance the second, more serious aspect of her personality: a sense of essential dissatisfaction, for deep down within Sandra, the worm of the *maudite vie plate,* the finite nature of the human condition itself, is gnawing away. She is quite aware of it in her moments of lucidity; it is this awareness that leads to the highly cynical tone of many of her speeches. Sandra has consciously chosen "la survie par le cul," the path of sexual excess, as a means to overcome existential anguish. She recognizes the shortcomings of her method. Many times, especially in unguarded moments such as right after awakening, her anguish comes to the surface: "C'est ben beau tout ça mais des fois en se réveillant, hein, on a beau se trouver potable, on sent comme un creux dans l'estomac... Y'a comme... de l'insatisfaction dans l'air" (37) ("That's all very well, but sometimes when you wake up, even if you find yourself quite tolerable, you get a sort of sinking feeling in your stomach... There is something like... dissatisfaction in the air").

These vague feelings of anxiety are reinforced by a very definite sense of lost identity. This is an issue which Sandra tries to avoid facing, but there are times when she can no longer fight the need to take off all her make-up, pull her long hair to the back of her head and expose her undisguised face to the mirror in an attempt to find her "real" self. However, the attempt invariably ends in total failure: "J'ai eu beau chercher, fouiller, scruter... j'me sus pas trouvé. Mon visage à moé existe pus.... Ça sert à rien d'essayer de me retrouver. J'existe pus. Me retrouver tout nu devant un miroir... me donne le vertige du néant! J'existe pus" (53–54) ("No matter how much I look, dig, scrutinize... I couldn't find myself. My real face doesn't exist any longer.... No point trying to find myself. I don't exist any longer. To find myself naked in front of a mirror means facing nothingness... it makes me dizzy! I don't exist any longer"). As Sandra well knows, her original self has been gradually driven out by the unending disguises she has superimposed on it; these have now taken over.

However, there is, as she (he!) points out with cynical

frankness, one part of her (him) that has never been disguised and which therefore remains as a single token of Sandra's identity: "Chus . . . resté ma queue. Tout le reste est accessoire" (54) ("There's nothing left of me but my tail. The rest doesn't matter"). Sexuality thus becomes not only the essence of Sandra's character but also the acknowledged motivating force of her life: "It's the tail that leads, I only execute orders." There is a profoundly tragic aspect to such a view of life, but Sandra refuses to dwell on it because "life is too short, and it seems to be getting shorter every day." She simply shrugs off the problem with good-natured laughter and moves on to the next erotic project. But even here, beneath the satisfaction afforded by her many professional triumphs, there lurks anger and disappointment. While she gloats over the number of her lovers, she knows very well that at bottom she is nothing for them but a "one, two or three star fuck." In a moment of rebellion, she goes off into an imagined orgy of violence in which she kills all her lovers and makes them into floor lamps, the better to light the way for their successors and fellow "pilgrims of sex." Despite her flippancy and humour, Sandra is not happy, and so she envies the presumed happiness of Manon, whose life she perceives as serene and untroubled.

Sandra's basic sensuality corresponds to the deep-seated spirituality that dominates Manon's character. Just as Sandra has spent a lifetime in the service of the senses, Manon has dedicated her entire life to the service of God. Just as Sandra has lost her original identity, so Manon's dedication to the religious life has changed her very appearance, to the extent that she is often taken for a nun. In fact, Tremblay has incarnated in the character of Manon all the features of the traditional mystic: the intensely personal relationship to God; the capacity for mystical ecstasy; and the experience of the "dark night of the soul," or divine eclipse. Manon's attitude is very much like that of the Old Testament patriarchs who freely conversed with God. She is convinced that the Lord has taken full charge of her life, signifying His will at every turn by "signs" which she alone can interpret. Thus, she gave up her life's most intense desire, that of becoming a nun, because God made it clear to her that her place is in the world and indeed on the rue Fabre, following in the footsteps of her saintly mother.

In one instance, the "divine will" manifests itself in a way that combines humour, pathos and ever-so-gentle satire: while bringing home her precious new rosary, Manon comes upon an empty garbage can at the bottom of which she notices a discarded old prayer book. This she immediately interprets as a sign that the Lord is telling her, like Abraham, to sacrifice that which is dearest to her by adding her new rosary to the prayer book in the garbage can. She duly makes the sacrifice, but as she stands by shaking with sobs, a neighbourhood urchin makes fun of her, and she grabs her bag again and runs home. Back in her room, she throws herself at the feet of her Virgin Mary and begs her to intercede. "Your son really goes too far sometimes!" Manon complains.

Like the characters in the Old Testament, Manon believes that her relationship with the Lord constitutes a covenant, and she does not hesitate to call the Almighty to order when she feels that He has failed in His obligations to her. Thus, she bitterly accuses Him for having allowed her erotic nightmare, and her recriminations become almost threatening:

Si vous êtes trop exigeant, dites-Vous ben que moé aussi, j'peux être exigeante! J'crois en Vous parce que Vous existez, mais j'crois en Vous aussi parce que Vous êtes bon! Parce qu'y faut que Vous soyez bon! Le rêve que Vous m'avez envoyé aujourd'hui n'était pas bon! Pis je le rejette! (52–53) (If You are going to be too demanding, tell Yourself that I, too, can be demanding! I believe in You because You exist, but I also believe in You because You are good! Because You have to be good! The dream You sent me today was not good! And I reject it!)

In her moments of despair, when she feels the Divine Presence receding from her and seeks in vain the mystical pleasures she used to know, Manon becomes demanding indeed: "J'ai droit à mes jouissances! J'y ai droit! Chus t'habituée, astheur! C'que vous me faisiez, j'aime ça pis j'veux que ça continue!" (58) ("I have a right to my pleasures! I have a right! I'm used to it now! I like it, what you used to do to me, and I want it to continue!"). Her assertion of her right to be loved represents a complete reversal of the traditional position of mystical literature, where it is God, not the soul, who makes the demand. However, her despair at such times parallels the desper-

ation of all the seekers after mystical union through the ages when they experience periods of aridity: "Si vous êtes une journée, une seule journée, sans venir me visiter, j'vous avertis, j'vas venir folle..." (58) ("If you don't come to visit me for a day, one single day, I warn you, I am going to go crazy...").
The feeling echoes the agonies of the traditional mystic.
Mechtild of Magdeburg, for example, expresses herself in almost identical terms: "One hour is too long for me. If you should be remote for me no more than a week and a day,/In hell I should prefer to stay, where I already am...."[7]

Similarly, Manon's struggle towards attainment of the supreme ecstasy, when the Divine Presence does make Itself felt, is expressed in a somewhat modernized version of the traditional terms of mystical literature. Compare Hugh of St. Victor's "I struggle with all my strength to hold it and not lose it. I struggle deliciously to prevent myself leaving this thing which I desire to embrace forever"[8] with Manon's "Pas trop vite! Pas trop vite! Trop vite, c'est pas mieux... Si j'ai le vertige, j'vas retomber pis toute va être à recommencer!... Ha! J'ai retrouvé mes ailes!" (64) ("Not too fast! Not too fast! Too fast is not better... If I get dizzy I shall fall, and it'll all have to start over again!... Ah! I've found my wings!").

Manon eventually reaches the heights to which she aspires, an experience brilliantly rendered by her breathtaking outburst, one long sentence filled with poetry, paradox and metaphor, soaring with a rhythm that sweeps the reader along the path of Manon's ecstasies:

J'plane. Dans Votre Ombre Immense!... Seule Votre Lumière à Vous, qui se goûte dans le noir le plus profond, dans les ténèbres les plus secrètes, qui déchire l'âme à grands coups de sabre, qui pourfend l'oeil, le fait éclater, l'ouvre et le ressuscite, seule Votre Lumière qui mord la peau pis qui laisse des traces comme des blessures, seule Votre Lumière fait exploser la Vérité, la seule Vérité, Votre Vérité, seule Votre Lumière à Vous est la bonne! (64) (I am floating. In Your immense shadow!... Only Your Light, which is felt in the deepest darkness, in the most secret shadows, which tears the soul as with a sword, which splits the eye, bursts it open, opens and revives it, only Your Light which bites into the skin and leaves marks like wounds, only Your Light makes the Truth explode, the only Truth, Your Truth, only Your Light is the right one!)

At the very end of Manon's monologue of mystical ecstasy, there occurs a shift in the level of reality which ultimately reveals both characters as fictions created in the mind of the poet. Towards the end of her long speech, she pleads with God to continue His blessings and to believe in her, "even if I have been invented by Michel." At this point Sandra, who has been following Manon's ecstasies, bursts in on the scene pleading to be taken along on her flight, for "I, too, do not exist. I, too, have been invented!"

And so the play ends with all opposites coming together, all contradictions resolved, as Manon and Sandra return to the crucible of the author's imagination whence they came, both of them testifying each in her own way to that "eternal hunger which shall never more be satisfied,"[9] which has also been the underlying motif of every one of Tremblay's works to date. With this play, the author has indeed closed the cycle of *Les Belles-Soeurs*.

CHAPTER EIGHT

The Great Beyond:
Mythopoeic Drama and Early Prose Narratives

The preceding chapters have dealt in detail with Michel Tremblay's major plays. Of his lesser-known dramas, two early works, *Les Socles* and *Les Paons* (to date untranslated), are interesting enough to warrant analysis. Mythopoeic in character, they are more closely related to his early fictional works than to his dramatic opus. Like *La Cité dans l'oeuf* and many of the tales in *Contes pour buveurs attardés,* they belong to the "third" world within the Tremblay universe, not the rue Fabre/Family nor the Main, but the Grand Ailleurs, the world of the Great Beyond. They testify to the tension between opposites so characteristic of Tremblay: realism versus fantasy, sensuality versus spirituality, the here and now versus the absolute.

Because they are so different in spirit, these plays also differ radically in dramatic technique from the works discussed so far. The language used is classical French; abstract settings replace the naturalistic milieus we have become used to, and the characters are all allegorical. The basic themes are religious, in the widest sense of that word: *Les Socles* deals with the human condition in relation to the absolute powers which govern the universe; *Les Paons* attempts to combine a myth of theogenesis, the achieving of divine status, with a particular version of the Goetterdaemmerung idea. The underlying tone is one of deepest pessimism — this is the obvious link with the more naturalistic plays. In Tremblay's spiritual world, eternal life is achieved through sin rather than through virtue: he takes seriously the serpent's promise to Adam and Eve, "eritis sicut deus." The path to the Great Beyond, which transcends mortality, lies through crime; the price of eternal life, however, is eternal suffering, for "the gods are criminals expiating their crimes."

Les Socles (*The Pedestals*) is a short play in the absurdist style of Beckett which will serve as a useful introduction to the more complex *Les Paons*. The stage metaphors are clear and easily understandable, similar to the metaphors of Beckett's *Play without Words*. The language is stylized, the characters allegorical. As the play opens, the audience faces an almost empty stage, occupied only by two very high pedestals on which stand the Father and the Mother. In unison, they recite their first, and only, long speech:

En dehors de nous, il n'y a rien. Rien n'existe. Le monde n'est rien. Nous sommes seuls. Et nous l'avons voulu ainsi. Nous avons voulu être le monde et nous le sommes... Enfermés depuis toujours nous vivons dans un monde que nous avons fait. En dehors de nous, il n'y a rien. Rien n'existe. Et nos enfants sont tels que nous les avons voulus. Et nos enfants... sont les monstres que nous avons voulu qu'ils soient. Notre maison est un enfer que nous avons bâti. Notre monde est un enfer que nous avons bâti. Notre maison est un enfer que nous avons bâti. Notre monde est un enfer que nous avons bâti.... [1] (Outside of us, there is nothing. Nothing exists. The world is nothing. We are alone. And we have wished it thus. We have wished to be the world, and we are the world... Imprisoned forever we live in a world which we have created. Outside of us, there is nothing. Nothing exists. And our children are such as we wished them to be. And our children... are the monsters we wished them to be. Our house is a hell which we have built. Our world is a hell which we have built. Our house is a hell which we have built. Our world is a hell which we have built....)

This first speech identifies the play very clearly with the ideological world of French existentialism, so that the absurdist style in which it evolves appears a logical choice.

After the Mother and Father finish their speech, the Children enter. They are divided into two groups, four boys and four girls. There is no attempt at individualization; on the contrary, each group speaks with one voice, and the speeches of the two groups are interchangeable. As the play progresses, it becomes clear that the Children are being kept in a state of subordination and imprisonment by the parents, who allow them only a glimpse of freedom through an occasionally opened window. The Children's thoughts alternate between resignation — "nous ne pouvons pas ne pas vouloir ce qu'ils veulent" ("we cannot not wish what they wish") — and rebellion — "il faut sortir de cette maison" ("we must get out of this house"). Eventually, they realize that their strength lies in unity. All eight Children cross the stage, their arms around each other; together, they attack the pedestals. However, they lack the strength to knock them over. They then try to help each other to climb up to the top in order to reach the Father and Mother, but they keep falling back down again. The play ends on a note of total defeat, with the eight Children rolling on the floor, "fighting among themselves like animals."

As a parable of the human condition, *Les Socles* exhibits an unrelieved pessimism. Man is not only a prisoner of a world that is hell itself but he is also constitutionally incapable of achieving the freedom he occasionally glimpses. The sense of impotence is total. Frustration becomes unbearable just because man does have a conception of liberation that he can never realize; like Sisyphus, he is condemned eternally to fail in his attempts to reach his goal. This problem of free will extends from man to the gods: the Father and Mother, all-powerful on their pedestals, are as much part of a fully closed, predetermined world as are the Children.

Obviously, the parable can be applied on a number of levels. *Les Socles* is clearly an absurdist play which deals with the unbearable limitations of the human condition; in this context, the parent figures represent God, fate or destiny. But it is also a cruel parable about the hell of family living, and the choice of protagonists — "Father," "Mother," "Children" — makes the allegory absolutely transparent. Finally, one could extend the symbolism to a political level: the Father (the State) and the Mother (the Church) are keeping the Children (the people of Quebec) in total subjugation. The Children are also too intimidated, too resigned or simply too ineffectual to overthrow those powers and achieve their independence.

In contrast to *Les Socles,* which is a short, simple and straightforward parable, *Les Paons* (*The Peacocks*) represents an ambitious, complex, full-length drama that attempts nothing less than the creation of new versions of the archetypal myths of the rise and eclipse of the gods. The play was unsuccessful when it was first performed at the National Arts Centre in Ottawa in May 1971, and has not been produced since. Tremblay himself considers it a "bad play." In spite of its many weaknesses, the most important of which is a failure to fuse the naturalistic element with the element of fantasy, the play remains extremely interesting from the thematic point of view and well warrants discussion.

Les Socles simply assumes the existence of the godlike parent figures; *Les Paons* attempts to answer the question of how these divinities achieved their tragic/exalted state. The subject of the play, then, is the road travelled by two human beings, Agnès and Jérémie, as they cross over from the finite world into infinity. The peacocks of the title symbolize the dual aspect of divinity: glory, expressed by the brilliance of colour that is typical of the peacock; and horror, conveyed by the screams and shrieks that the same bird emits. The production uses both colour and sound: light effects and a ceremonial robe made of peacock feathers provide the element of glory, and recordings of the horrible guttural screams of the peacock underline the element of gloom and suffering.

The play is divided into three tableaux. It begins on a realistic note, shifts to alternations between realism and fantasy, and ends on a note of complete fantasy. However, the two opposed worlds, the naturalistic and the fantastic, are not integrated into a whole, so that many of the transitions appear artificial. The play opens with a contrast between two different realities. Before the curtain rises, we hear a "frightful noise, terminated by long lamentations of the peacocks." As the horrible noise subsides, we are presented with an innocuous stage setting that gives the appearance of ordinary life at its most banal: a middle-aged couple are sitting in the living room having their after-dinner coffee. Agnès and Jérémie are baby-sitting their beloved grandchildren while their daughter is taking a vacation. Suddenly, the conversation takes an ominous turn:

JEREMIE: Et si nous commencions tout de suite? Et si nous commencions par ici, Agnès? Et si nous commencions par nos propres enfants?

AGNES: Tu crois qu'ils accepteront?

. . . .

JEREMIE: Ils n'auront pas le choix, ma chérie. C'est pour leur bien.[2]

(JEREMIE: What if we started right away? What if we started right here, Agnès? If we started with our own children?

AGNES: Do you think they will accept?

. . . .

JEREMIE: They won't have a choice, my darling. It is for their own good.)

Now light and sound effects add to the threatening impact of the dialogue: the peacock screams, the stage is bathed in red light, and an infernal noise fills the air. From this point on, "normal" dialogue alternates with speeches which obviously indicate that something serious and far beyond the concerns of daily living is about to take place. The ritual character of the impending event is stressed from the beginning. Agnès decides it is time to start: "Je vais me préparer pour la cérémonie" ("I shall make ready for the ceremony"). As she prepares to leave, the back wall of the room disappears, revealing a staircase and a "magnificent ceremonial robe" covered with peacock feathers. The connotations of the ritual are threefold: criminal, sexual and religious. While Agnès performs her ritual off-stage, Jérémie keeps up a running commentary on what is happening: "Ah, Agnès, combien grande est ta mission. Approche, lentement, pousse la porte. Comme ils sont beaux, Agnès. . . . Approche . . . encore . . . plus près . . . penche-toi. Agnès. Agnès. Tu pleures. Redresse-toi, Agnès, et frappe!" (Oh, Agnès, how very great is your mission. Go close, push the door open slowly. How beautiful they are, Agnès. . . . Closer . . . and closer still . . . bend down. Agnès. Agnès. You are crying. Rise, Agnès, and strike!"). To the accompaniment of the brutal sounds of a bloody massacre, Jérémie keeps on shouting "Strike, strike!" until, in a paroxysm of pleasure, he utters one last cry of deliverance and remains doubled over. The scene is then repeated, with the parts reversed. As Jérémie returns, having performed his part of the ritual, the ceremonial robe once more appears. Agnès takes up a position in front of it, on her knees, arms extended to heaven: "Je suis prête" ("I am ready").

The second tableau leaves the naturalistic world behind. It describes how Agnès and Jérémie assume the burden of divinity, symbolized by the peacock robes. This scene faintly echoes the Genesis story of Adam and Eve, as Agnès eagerly moves forward towards a new fate ("I shall wait for the doors of the Great Beyond to open before my destiny") while Jérémie hesitates, filled with fear and apprehension. Like Eve with the apple, Agnès tries to persuade Jérémie to follow in her footsteps on the way to godhead: "Viens, Jérémie, viens, c'est l'heure. Tu verras, ce sera facile" ("Come on, Jérémie, come on. It is time. You will see, it will be easy"). Still, Jérémie refuses to join her, for the price of immortality appears too high: "Nous avons assassiné nos enfants, Agnès, pour avoir droit à ces robes... Nous avons tué des millions d'enfants, Agnès, pour avoir droit à ces robes" ("We have killed our children, Agnès, to gain a right to these robes... We have killed millions of children to gain a right to these robes"). Although Agnès points out to him that it is too late now to turn back, Jérémie still resists, for he has suddenly realized the truth about the gods and the enormity of the suffering that lies ahead: "Nous sommes des meurtriers, nous avons gagné notre place dans le Grand Ailleurs en commettant des crimes immondes et nous devrons payer. Agnès! Les dieux sont des criminels! Agnès! Les dieux sont des criminels qui expient leurs crimes!" ("We are murderers, we have won our place in the Great Beyond by committing horrible crimes and we shall have to pay. Agnès! The gods are criminals! Agnès! The gods are criminals who expiate their crimes!").

The appearance of a fantastically arrayed High Priest of the Great Beyond seals the fate of Agnès and Jérémie. While Agnès still gloats over the fulfilment of her dreams ("we shall be gods, Jérémie!"), Jérémie now has a clear picture of what lies in store for them:

Les portes du Grand Ailleurs s'ouvrent et une foule d'êtres hideux, difformes, malades, mourants, se précipitera pour nous accueillir. Les dieux ... Le dieux se meurent, Agnès. Le dieux se meurent et ne mourront jamais. Ils sont condamnés à ne jamais mourir. Nous serons des dieux maintenant, condamnés à mourir éternellement, Agnès! (The gates of the Great Beyond open and a crowd of hideous, misshapen, sickly, dying creatures will press forward to welcome us. The gods ... The gods are dying, Agnès. The gods are dying, but they will never be dead. They are condemned to live forever. We shall be gods, now, condemned to be dying for all eternity, Agnès!)

However, this insight has come too late. As the High Priest beckons, Jérémie, like Agnès before him, kneels in front of the ceremonial robe that awaits him, arms extended to heaven: "Je suis prêt" ("I am ready").

For the third tableau, the stage is lit up in a rainbow of peacock colours—blue, green, turquoise. Agnès executes a ritual dance after which Jérémie covers her with the ceremonial robe; the High Priest does the same for Jérémie. Their rise to power is indicated by a recitation describing their new-found status. It is the same recitation we have already heard in *Les Socles:* "Outside of us, there is nothing. The world is nothing. We are alone." Agnès and Jérémie are on their way to becoming the eternal Father and Mother figures, and at the end of the play we see them on their pedestal. As they slowly turn their faces towards the public, a "beatific smile" is discernible on their lips, but their eyes remain "horribly sad." This final tableau would have provided a moving and eloquent ending. However, Tremblay has added another detail that detracts from the impact: as the two characters stand rigidly on their pedestal, a procession of grotesque figures, led by the High Priest, approaches carrying tiaras and sceptres, the insignia of their new dignity. This procession is accompanied by infernal noises, screaming and howling, while Agnès and Jérémie quietly recite their "Outside of us" creed. Clearly the author's propensity to end his works with a spectacular finale has here gotten somewhat out of hand.

From a technical point of view, *Les Paons* is definitely not a successful work for the theatre. However, it is a work that contributes essentially to our understanding of Michel Tremblay, and therefore it cannot be overlooked. More than any of the more conventional works, this play expresses the dichotomy between an elementary desire for transcendence and despair at the impossibility of fulfilling this desire. The perverse mythology of *Les Paons* carries heavy overtones of both Nietzsche and Wagner. If God is dead, then new gods will have to arise; and Tremblay creates them by a process of revaluation of values. Mass murder, not self-immolation, is the key to the Great Beyond—this is Tremblay's bold inversion of Christian doctrine! Eternal life then becomes a mordant mockery of itself: not life at all, but a death that never ends, a Teutonic and Wagnerian twilight of the gods which perpetuates itself for ever and ever. Tremblay has substituted an eschatology of despair for the Christian eschatology of hope. If we keep in mind that he is struggling against the powerful influence of a Catholic upbringing, his reaction appears neither surprising nor unusual. Loss of faith is an intellectual process which often does not carry over into the area of emotional life; and so a man is capable of raging quite irrationally against something he declares nonexistent. In Tremblay's case, the metaphysical frustration and rage leads to a re-creation of the rejected myths with all their tenets turned upside down. Such a negative view of the gods also corresponds better to the generally pessimistic world view of modern man. It is no longer possible to fit the traditional Christian concept of God as an all-loving father into the context of the world as we know it, which has Auschwitz and Hiroshima as identifying marks. Tremblay's gods create no such contradiction. They lay no claim to love or compassion. Our modern experience of holocaust bears out their dicta:

Our world is a hell which we have built . . . The world is nothing. We watch our children live. We look at our children as they hate, fight, and tear each other apart. We have wished it thus. . . . Our children lacerate each other, rip each other, bite each other; our children are dying. But they will never be dead. . . . The world is nothing. We look at it.

(*Les Socles*)

In a similar vein, the short stories collected in the volume *Contes pour buveurs attardés* (*Tales for Late-Night Drinkers*) and the novel *La Cité dans l'oeuf* (*The City in the Egg*) represent excursions into a nightmare world of grotesque myths and fantasy. Although of dubious literary quality, these works, like the mythopoeic plays, are important as illustrations of the "other" Tremblay whose presence is constantly felt beneath the surface of his more naturalistic works.

Contes pour buveurs attardés represents Tremblay's literary efforts during his adolescent years.[3] The stories were written before his linguistic "illumination" took place, and are therefore couched in classical French. The themes echo the conventional themes of fantastic literature, especially nineteenth-century Gothic. Altogether, these pieces give evidence of much talent and imagination, but lack originality and that firm grip on the material which Tremblay was to develop later. They merit our attention because they make us aware of the author's obsession with the night side of life as well as his desire to transcend man's threefold limitation of world, mind and body. In trying to breach this triple barrier, young Tremblay introduces us to a world of fantasy and nightmare. Horror and cruelty, rather than beauty and happiness, are the usual attributes of the world beyond which he manages to evoke.

Some of the stories follow traditional models, such as the Werewolf theme ("Angus ou la lune vampire," "Wolfgang, à son retour") and the Bluebeard theme ("La Treizième Femme du baron Klugg"). The frequent occurrence of Germanic names indicates a close kinship between these fantasies and the stories of the German Romantics. In keeping with the nineteenth-century tradition, Tremblay uses the licence of fantasy to justify occurrences that have no rational explanation but are simply presented to the reader as fact: one example is the story "Le Pendu" ("The Hanged Man"), in which a man hanged since evening comes back to life in the early hours of the morning and begins to swing wildly on his rope. When he eventually falls, his head rolls away from his body and is never found. The story of Circe concerns a similar, typically Romantic incident in which a sailor experiences for a brief moment life on a "nonexistent" island with a siren. In spite of their conventional framework, all of these stories illustrate the author's very personal preoccupation, his desire for the absolute and transcendent. The same concern is present, in a much subtler manner, in his later work.

Tremblay's mysticism comes to the surface in several of the early stories based on an assumed separation of soul and body. In these stories the soul either leads a separate existence from the body during life or else continues an independent existence after death. The overall tone of *Contes pour buveurs attardés* is similar to the tone of Gothic horror stories, with an occasional frightening excursion into pure sadism and cruelty (the torture of a mouse in "Gerblicht"; the torture of a girl in "Marie").

Two of the stories provide a connecting link to the motifs of the considerably more sophisticated novel, *La Cité dans l'oeuf*. In "L'Oeil de l'idole," we are introduced to the mysterious land of Paganka, the home of the "blue people" who worship the god M'ghara, and this setting appears again in the later novel. The short story "La Dernière Sortie de Lady Barbara" ("Lady Barbara's Last Outing") touches on another of the later themes. Here Tremblay first uses the theme of *Les Paons*, in which crime is the key to breaking out of human limitations. In this earlier story, the High Priest orders the narrator to kill Lady Barbara, who is a combination old witch and cosmic superpower, for only by committing the murder can he become one of the Initiated: "vous pourrez alors revêtir la robe blanche qui défie le Temps et la Mort" (54) ("you will then be able to don the white robe which defies time and death"). There is an element of youthful rebellion in this persistent desire to defy the ultimate realities of human life, Time and Space; but the mystical element in the later works testifies to the fact that some of that spirit of metaphysical revolt remains with Tremblay still. In *La Cité dans l'oeuf*, written in 1968, the main protagonist does indeed overcome Time and Space. This work is both a cosmic fantasy and an attempt to create an alternative to existing mythologies in order to explain the existence of evil in the universe.

La Cité dans l'oeuf is not, however, a successful novel. In spite of Tremblay's careful construction, the story tends to

leave the reader confused; moreover, since there are no characters in the realistic sense of the word, our sympathies are never
fully engaged. It is difficult to classify the work, beyond the
general description of "fantasy": it carries overtones of the
Gothic horror story but could also be interpreted either as a
description of a nightmare or drug trip or as a philosophical
exercise in creating a mythology that is more appropriate to the
pessimistic world view of modern man than any of the traditional religious myths.

The point of departure for the fantasy is simple: François
Laplante, an ordinary citizen of Montreal, gains access to a
mysterious, visionary City beyond the confines of planet earth,
through a strange, egg-shaped object endowed with magical
powers which his father brought back from Africa. François,
who is obsessed with the egg, holds it in his hands one moonlit
night when suddenly it begins to soften and absorb him into the
City within it — and so begins his adventure beyond Time and
Space. He travels through the mysterious City, ruled over by
fallen gods, and battles the powers of evil, but eventually he is
expelled and finds himself back on his Montreal porch, the egg
still in his hands.

The most interesting aspect of the novel is probably the
basic mythology that underlies the story. However, because
this mythology is worked into the structure of the book in bits
and pieces, the reader has difficulty seeing it as a totality. The
following reconstruction is based on a synthesis of a number of
details that appear at different times in the narration; the process of synthesis reveals a perfectly coherent mythology which,
though fantastic, combines philosophical insight with poetic
imagination. Certain parallels with existing myths of both East
and West will become immediately apparent.

Like many existing mythologies, Tremblay's posits a
happy age in the past, a dark present which threatens immi-
nent destruction, and the possibility of another happy age in
the future which will result from the appearance of a Saviour
figure. As François Laplante learns in the City, there was
once a time when the most beneficent of heavenly bodies, the
"green planet," the planet of Love, ruled the universe. Its
course seemed to indicate that it might even enter the solar

system of the earth. Gods and men rejoiced, and the gods descended upon earth to exert a benevolent influence which led to the rise of two magnificent civilizations, Atlantide and Terre de Mu. However, after an unexplained cosmic catastrophe, the green planet of universal Love was diverted from its course, giving the Moon, planet of Madness, an opportunity to take power. The result was universal chaos: revolt and struggle among the gods, and war between the two great civilizations. Earthquakes and flood marked the beginning of a new dark age. As the flood receded, new religions and civilizations arose, but they were characterized by madness: "des civilisations et des religions de la lune, fondées par des demi-dieux fous" (136) ("civilizations and religions of the Moon, founded by insane half-gods"). This is Tremblay's vision of the present; his description of the state of man for as far back as the beginning of the historical record is poetic but not unrealistic. It may be an exercise in mythologizing to claim that the world as we know it is governed by a demented cosmic power which in turn causes madness in all those under its rule, but to a large extent the allegory fits the facts.

Tremblay foresees the possibility of a return to the lost paradise of "serenity" through the appearance of a human Saviour figure strong enough to overcome the forces of evil and with a will to use his power in the exercise of true wisdom.

Within this scheme of things, the City represents the once splendid but now decayed abode of the gods, who remain there against their will. Once the gateway to the Great Beyond, the City has become a gloomy prison where the gods are condemned to a slow death (the twilight of the gods motif), unless redeemed by a human Saviour. The City is a symbol, then, of the universe as a whole, but not an entirely original symbol if we think of Augustine's City of God or the medieval concept of the Heavenly City. Through his magical egg, François Laplante is able to enter this extraterrestrial City where he meets the gods and other mythological beings of Tremblay's fantasy world. Again, these beings represent combinations, variations and permutations of characters from various mythologies, Eastern and Western, with a heavily Teutonic/Wagnerian emphasis.

In the centre of the City, enthroned in a palace of lead, reside the archetypal couple, God/Father and God/Mother, M'ghara and Ismonde. Once omnipotent, now they also must suffer the consequences of the Moon's fatal power. Outside the centre, the City is divided into quarters, each one the domain of a particular god, offspring of M'ghara and Ismonde. François first meets Ghô, a horrible dwarf who used to be the god of beauty but rebelled against his mother Ismonde and was therefore punished by being turned into a monster. His entire life is spent planning revenge; he represents the power of evil, and it is he who will bring about the ultimate downfall of all the gods and the final end of the City. Next François comes upon the crystal goddess Lounia. Her beauty of body is unsurpassed and her singing irresistible; but her head is disfigured and her reason gone. Next he is taken to the district of the twin war gods, Waptuolep-Anaghwalep, perhaps the most tragic figure in the entire configuration. The war gods never wanted to be born; they realize the horrors they bring upon the world and desire only one thing; to be allowed to die and by their death, end all wars. But it cannot be so, for war is the natural accompaniment of the madness brought into the universe: "Du fond du Grand Ailleurs, ils avaient supplié la déesse-mère de ne pas les mettre au monde, mais la guerre sévissait et il lui fallait des dieux" (144) ("From the depths of the Great Beyond, they had pleaded with the goddess/mother not to bring them into the world, but war was raging, and it required gods"). Finally, Wolftung appears, symbol of wisdom and dignity, a tall and "indescribably beautiful" figure robed in blue and with a plumed helmet on his egg-shaped head.

Each one of the gods pleads with François to save the City by killing the evil dwarf Ghô before it is too late; Ghô, on the other hand, tries to make François an accomplice in his infamous scheme of revenge.

The City is inhabited by a variety of other mythological creatures who all have one eerie characteristic in common: they are living chimeras, beings who transcend the normal distinction between animate and inanimate matter. Thus, the "hyena-birds" are giant stone gargoyles who come alive and provide transportation for François. The other kinds of beings who inhabit the City are frankly monstrous. Outside the City proper, François comes upon the Warugoth-Shalas, winged, triangular-shaped beasts with grotesque mouths in their bellies, who are symbols of crime and violence. To his horror, François recognizes himself in the Warugoth-Shalas. In addition, there is a group of female figures called Khjoens. They are goddesses of time, whose noisemaking keeps Time going—their disappearance means the end of the universe.

The mythological world of *La Cité dans l'oeuf* is based on a number of discernible sources. In the first place, the same element of Gothic/Romantic fantasy that appeared in the earlier collection of short stories also appears in the novel and accounts for the device whereby Tremblay presents the impossible or inexplicable as though it were reality. It also accounts for his disregard of the distinction between animate and inanimate states, and for another Romantic feature: the archaic and medieval settings. A strong Wagnerian influence complements the element of Romantic fantasy. When Tremblay wrote *La Cité dans l'oeuf*, he had just discovered Wagner, and almost unconsciously he transposed many elements of Teutonic mythology to the novel, most importantly the central motif of Goetterdaemmerung or the twilight of the gods. The Wagnerian influence is also clearly discernible in some of the names ("Wolftung" is purely Teutonic), in some of the language (there are even a few words quoted in German) and in the motif of the evil dwarf. To a lesser extent, Tremblay has also incorporated key elements of traditional Indo-European mythologies (the Golden Age; the Flood) as well as purely Christian motifs (Fall and Redemption; the Saviour concept; the Fallen Angel). All this is combined with a modern sense of revolt against suffering, and an equally modern need to escape from the absurdity of this world into a Beyond of some sort. In fact, the entire book could be interpreted as a struggle to retain some consciousness of religion and a Supreme Power. The difficulty for the reader lies in the fact that these various elements are poorly integrated; the novel seems eclectic and lacking in unity. In spite of a clearly defined point of view and a careful, systematic structure, the novel is weak because the material itself seems to break out from the technical organization imposed upon it.

The novel is elaborately but logically structured:

Introduction. (a) Author's presentation of the manuscript; (b) François Laplante senior's account of how he acquired the egg.

Part I: "Before." (a) François Laplante junior given the egg at age twelve; (b) strange adventure, nightmare, related to the egg; (c) strange adventures, vision of the City, related to the egg.

Part II. (a) The City entrance gained; description of the City; (b) Ghô's district; (c) Lounia's district; (d) Anaghwalep-Waptuolep's district; (e) Wolftung's district; (f) Ismonde and M'ghara.

Epilogue. Back in Montreal, experiences of next full moon.

The story develops along this clear outline but is interrupted by irregular interpolations, brief passages which break the logical sequence and take us across time and space. These passages reinforce the impression that we are witnessing either dream sequences or hallucinations brought about in an overexcited mind by the influence of the full moon.

La Cité dans l'oeuf is without a doubt the work of a human being in supreme anguish. It creates a whole new mythology in an attempt to revolt against the God who has let us down by not existing; it is, in other words, a testament of the crisis of faith of modern man.

Before embarking on his mystical voyage into the City within the egg, François Laplante experiences an existentialist anguish which leaves him feeling, knowing, demanding that there should be other worlds beyond what we know—which is nothing. The protagonist no doubt expresses the feelings of the author himself in this passage, which must be quoted at some length:

ce soir-là, le ciel était si pur, si transparent que je sentis pour la première fois de ma vie sa profondeur, ses dimensions incroyables. Je vis de mes yeux, et cela me bouleversa, que la lune n'était pas accrochée à un morceau de velours, et que derrière elle, la vide continuait, sans fin! SANS FIN! Je réalisai alors toute l'horreur de l'univers, de cette

création infinie dont on ne sait rien et dont on ne saura jamais rien.
J'avais fait de moi le monde et le monde n'était rien! Et j'ai senti...
les autres mondes, tous les autres mondes eloignés et perdus eux
aussi, avec des êtres différents de moi, monstrueux pour moi qui étais
un monstre pour eux!... Soudain je me mis à trembler à la pensée
qu'il n'y avait peut-être pas d'autres mondes... Non! Il fallait
absolument qu'il y eut d'autres mondes! Je ne voulais pas être seul
dans l'univers!... (53) (that evening, the sky was so pure, so transparent, that I felt for the first time in my life its depth, its incredible
dimensions. I saw with my own eyes that the moon was not something attached to a velvet backdrop, and I was overwhelmed — beyond
the moon, emptiness continued, without end! WITHOUT END! I
realized the full horror of the universe, of this infinite creation of
which we know nothing and will never know anything. I had made of
myself the world, and the world was nothing! And I felt... the other
worlds, all the other worlds, far away and lost also, with beings
different from me, monstrous for me who was a monster for
them!... Suddenly I began to tremble at the thought that perhaps
there were no other worlds... No! There simply had to be other
worlds! I did not want to be alone in the universe!...)

The voyage through the City within the egg provides him
with a glimpse of those other worlds; but it is still not enough.
Those worlds are subject to the same laws of impermanence as
ours. And so, in his final prayer, François calls out to the
hidden God — no doubt the God of his childhood — to come to
his rescue: "Dieu Tout-Puissant, vous qui dirigez la destinée de
la Création entière, vous que M'ghara lui-même appelait à son
secours dans son palais de plomb, SI VOUS EXISTEZ
QUELQUE PART, AYEZ PITIE DE MOI!" (182) ("Almighty God, You who direct the destiny of the entire Creation,
You whom M'ghara himself called to his aid in his lead palace,
IF YOU EXIST SOMEWHERE, HAVE PITY ON
ME!").

Certainly, the novel can be interpreted as an imaginative
escape from the anguish of everyday living into a world of fantasy. It can also be seen as the natural result of the writer's preoccupation with comparative religion and mythology. But first
and foremost, it must be seen as a document recording a crisis of
faith, specifically the author's rebellion against the Christian

faith of his childhood. In the list of "grands initiés," the wise men and prophets from ancient times to the present, Tremblay includes the wisdom of East and West but omits the name of Jesus from among the great moral leaders of mankind. However, the extent of the rebellion indicates the extent of the need for that which is rebelled against. *La Cité dans l'oeuf*, indifferent as a novel, serves an important purpose in alerting us to the significant mystical dimension in all the work of Michel Tremblay.

In *Damnée Manon, Sacrée Sandra,* Sandra the transvestite sensualist turns out to be little "Michel" grown up; but let us not be deceived. The author's deepest feelings are with Manon the mystic: "Manon, c'est moi!" ("I am Manon!"), as he himself has said. The mystic cannot exist without the sensualist and vice versa, nor can Tremblay's work be understood without an awareness of a similar duality in his personality and his literary viewpoint.

Notes

Chapter One

1. In an interview with Martial Dassylva, "Quand Michel Tremblay traite de fanatisme en religion et sexe," *La Presse* (Montreal), 26 février 1977.

2. *A toi, pour toujours, ta Marie-Lou* in 1972; *En pièces détachées* in 1973 and 1974; *Les Belles-Soeurs* in 1973; *Hosanna* in 1974; *Bonjour, là, bonjour* in 1975; *Surprise! Surprise!* in 1975.

3. Fernand Doré, "Michel Tremblay, le gars à barbe sympathique," *Magazine Maclean,* juin 1969, p. 60.

4. Lise Gauvin, "Littérature et langue parlée au Québec," *Etudes françaises* 10, no. 1 (février 1974) : 85.

5. Yerri Kempf, *Les Trois Coups à Montréal* (Montreal: Déom, 1965), p. 31.

6. Jules Audet, "Notre Parole en liberté," *Incidences,* no. 10 (août 1966).

7. Jean-Claude Germain, "Michel Tremblay, le plus joual des auteurs ou vice-versa," *Digeste-Eclair,* octobre 1968, p. 15.

8. A term used by Gilbert David in "Notes dures sur un théâtre mou," *Etudes françaises* 11, no. 2 (mai 1975):95.

9. See Michel Bélair, *Le Nouveau Théâtre québécois* (Montreal: Leméac, 1973).

10. The most important series broadcast by Radio-Canada were "Tableaux Canadiens" (1946), "Radio-Théâtre" (beginning in 1944) and "Nouveautés Dramatiques" (beginning in 1950).

11. Spoken by the character of the doctor, Olivier, in *Les Beaux Dimanches*.

12. Claude Jasmin, "L'Importance de se trouver une identité," *Lettres et écritures* 2, no. 1 (novembre 1964):16.

Chapter Two

1. *La Barre du jour,* nos. 3-5 (juillet-décembre 1965).

2. In G. Anthony, ed., *Stage Voices: Twelve Canadian Playwrights Talk about Their Lives and Work* (Toronto: Doubleday Canada, 1978), p. 282.

3. Jacques Languirand, "Le Québec et l'américanité," in *Klondyke* (Ottawa: Cercle du Livre de France, 1971), p. 232.

4. André Brassard, interviewed in *L'Envers du décor, périodique du Théâtre du Nouveau Monde* 10, no. 7 (mai-juin 1978):5.

5. *Les Paons* is unpublished; *Les Socles* appeared in both French and English in the *Canadian Theatre Review,* Fall 1979.

6. In an interview with Renate Usmiani, *Canadian Theatre Review,* Fall 1979, p. 29.

7. Michel Tremblay, "Témoignages sur le théâtre québécois," in *Le Théâtre canadien-français,* Archives des lettres canadiennes, vol. 5 (Montreal: Fides, 1976), p. 791.

8. Interviewed in *Nord* 1, no. 1 (automne 1971): 64.

9. Ben-Ami Scharfstein, *Mystical Experience* (Baltimore: Penguin Books, 1973), p. 1.

10. Michel Tremblay, *Contes pour buveurs attardés* (Montreal: Editions du Jour, 1966), p. 59.

11. For this reason, the English translations provided in this book are the author's own.

12. Quoted in Michel Bélair, *Michel Tremblay* (Montreal: Presses de l'université du Québec, 1972), p. 88.

Chapter Three

1. Martial Dassylva, "L'Amour du joual et des timbres-poste," *La Presse* (Montreal), 29 août 1968.

2. Georges-Henri D'Auteuil, S.J., "Théâtre," *Relations* 28, no. 331

(1968) : 287.

3. Naim Kattan, "Le Théâtre à Montréal," *Canadian Literature,* Spring 1969, p. 45.

4. Jaques Cellard, "Les Belles-Soeurs, quinze femmes du Québec," *Le Monde* (Paris), 25–26 novembre 1973, p. 19.

5. Interviewed in *Magazine Maclean,* février 1969, p. 30.

6. Tremblay himself has explained the somewhat astounding finale as follows: by dutifully rising and joining in the singing of "O Canada," Germaine regains the favour of the powers above — so it is only natural that the heavens should open and release their bounty for her once more. This tongue-in-cheek explanation should help to silence those who maintain that Tremblay lacks a sense of humour!

7. It is impossible to give a full English equivalent of the French "maudite vie plate" and its multilevelled connotations: "rotten, dull, uninteresting, empty, meaningless life" is a beginning.

8. Interviewed in *Nord* 1, no. 1 (automne 1971) : 69.

9. For a thinly disguised description of the environment of Michel Tremblay's youth, see especially his play *Bonjour, là, bonjour* and his novel *La Grosse Femme d'à côté est enceinte.*

10. C.J. Jung, *Les Métamorphoses de l'âme et ses symboles* (Geneva, 1953), p. 317.

11. In an interview with Michel Beaulieu, *Perspectives,* 17 février 1973, p. 6.

12. Ibid.

Chapter Four

1. In G. Anthony, ed., *Stage Voices: Twelve Canadian Playwrights Talk about Their Lives and Work* (Doubleday Canada, 1978), p. 282.

2. Margaret Atwood, *Survival* (Toronto: House of Anansi Press, 1972), p. 131.

3. See Jean Bergeron, *L'Agriculture et l'église, deux amies intimes d'origine divine* (Quebec: Librairie de l'action catholique, 1944).

4. Pierre Vallières, *Nègres blancs d'Amérique* (Paris: F. Maspéro, 1969), p. 88.

5. Jacques Cotnam, "Du Sentiment national dans le théâtre qué-

bécois," in *Le Théâtre canadien-français,* Archives des lettres canadiennes, vol. 5 (Montreal: Fides, 1976), p. 367.

6. For a complete production history of *En pièces détachées*, see Bibbliography. The discussion of the play in this chapter is based on Leméac's 1972 edition, which is the television version. It is slightly streamlined from the stage version, the most important change being the elimination of the first scene, the "duo" of the sandwich-board men.

7. In an interview with Gilles Marsolais, *Cahiers de la Nouvelle Compagnie Théâtrale,* 1 octobre 1974, p. 25.

8. Ibid.

9. Ibid, p. 27.

10. Paule Baillargeon, interviewed in *Stratégie,* no. 9 (été 1974) : 36.

Chapter Five

1. In G. Anthony, ed., *Stage Voices: Twelve Canadian Playwrights Talk about Their Lives and Work* (Toronto: Doubleday Canada, 1978), p. 283.

2. Jan Kott, *Shakespeare, Our Contemporary* (New York: W.W. Norton & Co., 1974), p. 105.

3. Margaret Atwood, *Survival* (Toronto: House of Anansi Press, 1972), p. 199.

4. Jacques Lazure, "Les Affinités du Québec avec la Nouvelle Culture," in Ghislaine Houle and Jacques Lafontaine, *Ecrivains québécois de Nouvelle Culture,* Bibliographies québécoises, no. 2 (Montreal: Ministère des Affaires Culturelles du Québec, 1975), p. xxvi.

5. In G. Anthony, ed., *Stage Voices,* p. 284.

Chapter Six

1. In an interview with Gilles Marsolais, *Cahiers de la Nouvelle Compagnie Théâtrale,* 1 octobre 1974, p. 26.

2. Micheline Cambron, "Michel Tremblay: *Sainte Carmen de la Main,*" *Livres et auteurs québécois,* 1976, p. 198.

3. Michel Tremblay, "A chacun son Godot," *L'Envers du décor, périodique du Théâtre du Nouveau Monde* 10, no. 7 (mai-juin 1978).

Chapter Seven

1. In an interview with Martial Dassylva, "Quand Michel Tremblay traite de fanatisme en religion et sexe," *La Presse* (Montreal), 26 février 1977.

2. For further insights into this aspect of Michel Tremblay, see his statements in an interview with the author, *Canadian Theatre Review,* Fall 1979, p. 34.

3. In connection with the novels of J.-C. Harvey. Gilles Marcotte, *Une Littérature qui se fait* (Montreal: Editions HMH, 1962), p. 24.

4. Jacques Languirand, "Le Québec et l'américanité," in *Klondyke* (Ottawa: Cercle du Livre de France, 1971), p. 231.

5. Pierre Vallières, *Nègres blancs d'Amérique* (Paris: F. Maspéro, 1969), p. 84.

6. In an interview with Martial Dassylva, "Quand Michel Tremblay traite de fanatisme en religion et sexe," *La Presse* (Montreal), 26 février 1977.

7. Quoted in H.A. Reinhold, ed., *The Soul Afire* (New York: Pantheon Books, 1944), p. 273.

8. Ibid., p. 238.

9. John Ruysbroek, quoted in Paul de Jaegher, ed., *An Anthology of Mysticism* (Westminster, Md., 1950), p. 49.

Chapter Eight

1. Quotations from *Les Socles* are based on the manuscript version made available to the author by Michel Tremblay.

2. *Les Paons* is an unpublished play. Quotations are based on the manuscript version made available to the author by the Centre d'Essai des Auteurs Dramatiques, Montreal.

3. According to Tremblay, dates given for individual stories in the collection published by Editions du Jour should be advanced by about three years to correspond to the actual dates of composition.

Chronology

1942   Born 25 June on rue Fabre, East Montreal, son of Armand Tremblay, a linotype operator, and Rhéauna Tremblay.

1955   Wins a scholarship to attend a *collège classique,* as the "best in French" student of the province, but returns to public school soon afterward, in protest against the "snobbism" he meets at the *collège classique.*

1959   Becomes a linotype operator.

1964   *Le Train,* written in 1959, wins first prize in Radio-Canada's Young Authors' Competition.

1970   *Les Belles-Soeurs* wins "Best play."

1972   *A toi, pour toujours, ta Marie-Lou* wins "Best play."

1973–76   Receives annual Chalmers Award.

1974   Wins the Prix Victor-Morin.

1975   Wins the Canadian Film Festival's "Best screenplay" for *Françoise Durocher, Waitress.*

1976   Awarded the Lieutenant-Governor's Medal, Ontario.

1977   Awarded the Lieutenant-Governor's Medal, Ontario.

Bibliography

I. By Tremblay

A. Plays and First Productions

1964 *Le Train.*

A one-act play written in 1960; it won first prize in Radio-Canada's Young Authors' Competition in 1964. Unpublished.

1965 *Messe noire.*

The Mouvement Contemporain troupe, directed by André Brassard, adapted several of the *Contes pour buveurs attardés* for dramatic recital at the Théâtre du Gesú, Montreal.

1966 *Cinq.*

Six one-act plays, performed by the Mouvement Contemporain troupe, directed by André Brassard. Two of the sketches were later replaced by two new ones and the series became *En pièces détachées* (see below). The two earliest sketches, *Berthe* and *Johnny Mangano and His Astonishing Dogs,* were used with a third sketch, *Gloria Star,* to become *Trois Petits Tours* (see Works for Film and Television).

1968 *Les Belles-Soeurs.* 2nd ed. Montreal: Leméac, 1972.

Written in 1965; performed in August 1968 by the Théâtre du Rideau Vert, Montreal, directed by André Brassard. First published by Holt, Rinehart & Winston in 1968.

1969 *En pièces détachées.* 2nd ed. Montreal: Leméac, 1972.

New version of *Cinq* (see above). Performed in April, directed by André Brassard. First published by Leméac in 1970, with *La Duchesse de Langeais.*

1969   *La Duchesse de Langeais.* 2nd ed. Montreal: Leméac, 1973.

Performed in Spring 1969 at Val-d'Or by Les Insolents, directed by Hélène Bélanger. Performed in March 1970 at the Théâtre de Quat'Sous, Montreal, under the direction of André Brassard. First published by Leméac in 1970, with *En pièces détachées.* Published in 1973 with *Hosanna.*

1970   *Demain matin, Montréal m'attend* (1st version).

Musical comedy performed at the Jardin des Etoiles à la Ronde, Montreal. Directed by André Brassard, music by François Dompierre.

1971   *A toi, pour toujours, ta Marie-Lou.* Montreal: Leméac, 1971.

Performed in April at the Théâtre de Quat'Sous, Montreal, directed by André Brassard.

1971   *Les Paons.*

A one-act fantasy performed by L'Atelier d'Ottawa. Unpublished.

1972   *Demain matin, Montréal m'attend* (2nd version). Montreal: Leméac, 1972.

Performed in March at Place des Arts, Montreal. Directed by André Brassard, music by François Dompierre.

1973   *Hosanna.* Montreal: Leméac, 1973.

Performed in May at the Théâtre de Quat'Sous, Montreal, directed by André Brassard. Published with *La Duchesse de Langeais.*

1973   *Les Belles-Soeurs.*

Performed November to December in Paris; best foreign play of the year. Performed November to December at Place des Arts, Montreal, under the direction of André Brassard.

1974   *Bonjour, là, bonjour.* Montreal: Leméac, 1974.

Performed in August at the National Arts Centre, Ottawa, and September to October in Montreal; directed by André Brassard.

1975   *Surprise! Surprise!* Montreal: Leméac, 1977.

Performed in April by the Théâtre du Nouveau Monde, Montreal, directed by André Brassard. Published with *Damnée Manon, Sacrée Sandra.*

1976   *Les Héros de mon enfance*. Montreal: Leméac, 1976.

Musical comedy performed in June at the Théâtre de Marjolaine, Eastman, Quebec. Directed by Gaétan Labrèche, music by Sylvain Lelièvre.

1976   *Sainte Carmen de la Main*. Montreal: Leméac, 1976.

Performed in July and September at Place des Arts, Montreal, directed by André Brassard.

1977   *Damnée Manon, Sacrée Sandra*. Montreal: Leméac, 1977.

Performed in October at the Théâtre de Quat'Sous, Montreal, directed by André Brassard. Published with *Surprise! Surprise!*

1978   *Sainte Carmen de la Main*.

Performed May to June by the Théâtre du Nouveau Monde, Montreal, directed by André Brassard.

B. English-Language Translations and First Productions

1972   *Forever Yours Marie-Lou*. Translated by John Van Burek and Bill Glassco. Vancouver: Talonbooks, 1975.

Performed in November at the Tarragon Theatre, Toronto, directed by Bill Glassco.

1973   *Like Death Warmed Over (En pièces détachèes)*. Translated by Allan Van Meer. Toronto: Playwrights Co-op, 1973.

Performed in January at the Warehouse, Manitoba Theatre Centre, Winnipeg, under the direction of André Brassard.

1973   *Les Belles-Soeurs*. Translated by John Van Burek and Bill Glassco. Vancouver: Talonbooks, 1974.

Performed in April at the St. Lawrence Centre, Toronto, directed by André Brassard.

1974   *Montreal Smoked Meat (En pièces détachées*. Translated by Allan Van Meer. Vancouver: Talonbooks, 1975.)

Performed 5 March to 15 April at the New Theatre, Toronto, directed by Jonathan Stanley.

1974   *Broken Pieces (En pièces détachées*. Translated by Allan Van Meer. Vancouver: Talonbooks, 1975.)

Performed 10 October to 9 November at the Arts Club Theatre, Vancouver, directed by Bill Millerd.

1974 *Hosanna.* Translated by John Van Burek and Bill Glassco. Vancouver: Talonbooks, 1974.

Performed in May and September at the Tarragon Theatre, Toronto, directed by Bill Glassco. Performed in November at the Bijou, New York, by Tarragon Productions.

1975 *Bonjour, là, bonjour.* Translated by John Van Burek and Bill Glassco. Vancouver: Talonbooks, 1975.

Performed February to March at the Tarragon Theatre, Toronto, directed by Bill Glassco.

1975 *Surprise! Surprise!* In *La Duchesse de Langeais and Other Plays.* Translated by John Van Burek. Vancouver: Talonbooks, 1976.

Performed October to November at the St. Lawrence Centre, Toronto, by Toronto Arts Productions. Directed by Eric Steiner.

1978 *Sainte Carmen of the Main.* Translated by John Van Burek. Vancouver: Talonbooks, 1978.

Performed January to February at the Tarragon Theatre, Toronto, directed by André Brassard.

1978 *Damnée Manon, Sacrée Sandra.* Translated by John Van Burek. Vancouver: Talonbooks, 1981.

Translated and adapted by Renate Usmiani and John Brown. Performed in November at Mount Saint Vincent University, Halifax.

C. Novels and Short Stories

1966 "Manoua." *La Barre du jour,* January–February, pp. 29-30. (Short story.)

1966 *Contes pour buveurs attardés.* Montreal: Editions du Jour. (Short stories.)

1969 *La Cité dans l'oeuf.* Montreal: Editions du Jour. (Novel.)

1973 *C't'à ton tour, Laura Cadieux.* Montreal: Editions du Jour. (Novel.)

1978 *Stories for Late Night Drinkers.* Translated by Michael Bullock. Vancouver: Intermedia Press.

1978 *La Grosse Femme d'à côté est enceinte.* Montreal: Leméac. (Novel.)

D. Adaptations/Translations

1969   *Lysistrata,* by Aristophanes. Montreal: Leméac, 1969.

Performed in May at the National Arts Centre, Ottawa, by the Théâtre du Nouveau Monde. Directed by André Brassard.

1970   *L'Effet des rayons gamma sur les vieux-garçons* (*The Effect of Gamma Rays on Man-in-the-Moon Marigolds,* by Paul Zindel). Montreal: Leméac, 1970.

Performed in September at the Théâtre de Quat'Sous, Montreal, directed by André Brassard.

1972   *Et Mademoiselle Roberge boit un peu* (*And Miss Reardon Drinks a Little,* by Paul Zindel). Montreal: Leméac, 1971.

Translation and adaptation.

1972   *Au pays du dragon* (four one-act plays by Tennessee Williams).

Translation and adaptation. Performed at the Théâtre de Quat'Sous, Montreal, directed by André Brassard.

1973   *mistero buffo,* by Dario Fo.

Translation and adaptation. Performed in December at the Théâtre du Nouveau Monde, Montreal, directed by André Brassard.

1976   *Mademoiselle Marguerite* (*Aparaceu a Margarida,* by Roberto Athayde). Montreal: Leméac, 1975.

Translation and adaptation. Performed in February at the National Arts Centre, Ottawa, and in March at the Théâtre du P'tit Bonheur, Toronto. Directed by Jean Dalmain.

E. Works for Film and Television

1969   *Trois Petits Tours.* Montreal: Leméac, 1971.

Three sketches, *Berthe, Johnny Mangano and His Astonishing Dogs* and *Gloria Star,* broadcast on 21 December on the French-language CBC television network in the series "Les Beaux Dimanches." Produced by Paul Blouin. Rebroadcast on 22 August 1971.

1971   *En pièces détachées.* Montreal: Leméac, 1972.

Produced on 6 March in the French-language CBC-TV series

"Les Beaux Dimanches" by Paul Blouin. Rebroadcast on 23 July 1972.

1972 *Françoise Durocher, Waitress.*

Short National Film Board production, directed by André Brassard. Broadcast on 8 October on the French-language CBC-TV network.

1972 *Backyard Theatre.*

National Film Board production about Tremblay and André Brassard, with characters from *Les Belles-Soeurs* and *Demain matin, Montréal m'attend.*

1974 *Il était une fois dans l'est.* Montreal: L'Aurore, 1974.

Film co-written and directed by André Brassard. An official Canadian entry at the Cannes festival in May. Distributed by Ciné/Art, Montreal.

1975 *Le Soleil se lève en retard.*

Film directed by André Brassard. Broadcast in Spring 1979 on the French-language CBC-TV network. Distributed by Films 16, Montreal.

1975 *Parlez-nous d'amour.*

Film directed by Jean-Claude Lord. Distributed by Films 16, Montreal.

1977 *Bonheur d'occasion,* by Gabrielle Roy.

Adapted for television.

1978 *Les Belles-Soeurs.*

Broadcast in March on the English-language CBC-TV network.

II. Secondary Sources

A. ABOUT TREMBLAY

Anthony, G., ed. *Stage Voices: Twelve Canadian Playwrights Talk about Their Lives and Work.* Toronto: Doubleday Canada, 1978.

Beaulieu, Michel. Interview. *Perspectives,* 17 février 1973, p. 6.

Bélair, Michel. *Michel Tremblay.* Montreal: Presses de l'université du Québec, 1972.

Berubé, Renald. *"Demain matin, Montréal m'attend,* de Michel Tremblay." *Livres et auteurs québécois,* 1976, p. 116.

Bibliography of interviews with Michel Tremblay. *Etudes françaises* 10, no. 1 (février 1974):84–85.

Brabant, Madeleine. *"En pièces détachées* de Michel Tremblay: Une étude de moeurs tragiques." *Ici Radio-Canada* 5, no. 11 (1971):3.

Cloutier, Rachel; Laberge, Marie; and Gignac, Rodrique. Interview. *Nord* 1, no. 1 (automne 1971):68–78.

Dassylva, Martial. "Quand Michel Tremblay traite de fanatisme en religion et en sexe." *La Presse,* 26 février 1977.

D'Auteuil, Georges-Henri, S.J. "Théâtre." *Relations* 28, no. 331 (1968):286.

David, Gilbert. "Notes dures sur un théâtre mou." *Etudes françaises* 9, no. 2 (mai 1975):95–109.

Gélinas, Marc F. "Je pense en joual." *Magazine Maclean,* septembre 1970, p. 46.

Germain, Jean-Claude. "Michel Tremblay, le plus joual des auteurs ou vice-versa." *Digeste-Eclair,* octobre 1968, p. 15.

Godin, Jean-Cleo. *"La Duchesse de Langeais,* de Michel Tremblay." *Livres et auteurs québécois,* 1970, p. 83.

Godin, Jean-Cleo, and Mailhot, Laurent. *Le Théâtre québécois.* Montreal: Editions HMH, 1970.

Guay, Jacques. "Guichet fermé." *Magazine Maclean,* février 1969, p. 30.

Joly, Raymond. "Une Douteuse Libération." *Etudes françaises* 8, no. 4 (1972):363–74.

———. *"Hosanna, La Duchesse de Langeais,* de Michel Tremblay." *Livres et auteurs québécois,* 1972, p. 160.

Kattan, Naim. "Le Théâtre à Montréal." *Canadian Literature,* Spring 1969, p. 45.

Laroche, Maximilien. *"Les Belles-Soeurs,* de Michel Tremblay," *Livres et auteurs canadiens,* 1968, p. 71.

Leroux, Normand. "Le Théâtre en 1968." *Livres et auteurs canadiens,* 1968, p. 64.

McQuaid, Catherine. "Michel Tremblay's Seduction of the Other Solitude." *Canadian Drama* 2, no. 2 (1976):217–21.

Mailhot, Laurent. "Les Belles-Soeurs ou l'enfer des femmes." *Etudes françaises,* février 1970, p. 96

————. "Pour l'amour du bonjour." Preface to *Bonjour, là, Bonjour,* by Michel Tremblay. Montreal: Leméac, 1974.

Marsolais, Gilles. "Michel Tremblay parle de. . . . " *Cahiers de la Nouvelle Compagnie Théâtrale,* 1 octobre 1974.

Ryngaert, J.P. "Du réalisme à la théâtralité: La dramaturgie de Michel Tremblay dans *Les Belles-Soeurs* et *A toi, pour toujours, ta Marie-Lou.*" *Livres et auteurs québécois,* 1971, p. 97.

Smith, André. "Michel Tremblay: *Bonjour, là, bonjour.*" *Livres et auteurs québécois,* 1974, p. 158.

Thério, Adrien. "Un Joual fringant à la scène en 1968." *Livres et auteurs canadiens,* 1968, p. 78.

Tremblay, Michel. "Témoignages sur le théâtre québécois." In *Le Théâtre canadien-français.* Archives des lettres canadiennes, vol. 5. Montreal: Fides, 1976, pp. 789–93.

Turcotte, André. "Les Belles-Soeurs en revolte." *Voix et images du pays* 3 (1970):183.

Usmiani, Renate. "Michel Tremblay's 'Sainte Carmen': Synthesis and Orchestration." *Canadian Drama* 2, no. 2 (1976):206–18.

Villemaire, Yolande. "Les Pouvoirs de la parole." *Cahiers de la Nouvelle Compagnie Théâtrale* 9, no. 1 (octobre 1974).

B. General Works on French-Canadian Literature and Civilization

Atwood, Margaret. *Survival.* Toronto: House of Anansi Press, 1972.

Bergeron, Jean. *L'Agriculture et l'église, deux amies intimes d'origine divine.* Quebec: Librairie de l'action catholique, 1944.

Gagnon, Gabriel, and Martin, Luc, comps. *Québec 1960–1980, la crise du développement.* Montreal: Editions HMH, 1973.

Gobin, Pierre. *Le Fou et ses doubles.* Presses de l'université de Montréal, 1978.

Jasmin, Claude. "L'Importance de se trouver une identité." *Lettres et écritures* 2, no. 1 (novembre 1964).

Lamontagne, Léopold. *Le Canada français d'aujourd'hui: Etudes rassemblées par la Société Royale du Canada, 1967.* Quebec: Presses de l'université Laval, 1970.

Memmi, Albert. *Portrait du colonisé.* Paris: Petite bibliothèque Payot, 1973.

Moisan, Clément. *L'Age de la littérature canadienne.* Montreal: Editions HMH, 1969.

Pontaut, Alain. *Dictionnaire critique du théâtre québécois.* Montreal: Leméac, 1972.

Scott, Frank, and Oliver, Michael. *Quebec States Her Case.* Toronto: Macmillan Company of Canada, 1964.

Vallières, Pierre. *Nègres blancs d'Amérique.* Paris: F. Maspéro, 1969.

C. Discussions of the Problem of the French Language in Quebec

Allard, Jacques. "Dix Remarques sur la vie de la langue française au Québec." *Europe* 47, nos. 478-79 (février-mars 1969):21-23.

Bouthilier, Guy, and Meynaud, Jean. *Le Choc des langues au Québec.* Montreal: Presses de l'université du Québec, 1972.

Charest, Gilles. *Le Livre des sacres et blasphèmes québécois.* Montreal: L'Aurore, 1974.

Gauvin, Lise. "Littérature et langue parlée au Québec." *Etudes françaises* 10, no. 1 (février 1974):80-84.

————. *Parti Pris littéraire.* Montreal: Presses de l'université de Montréal, 1975.

Gélinas, Gratien. "Pour un théâtre national et populaire." In *Gratien Gélinas*, by Renate Usmiani. Toronto: Gage Publishing, 1974.

STUDIES IN CANADIAN LITERATURE began in 1969 as a series of critical overviews designed to give students and general readers better access to significant Canadian writing. Now under the general editorship of Gary Geddes, it is a continuing forum for analysis of the work of important Canadian authors both established and experimental.